ABORTION

The Essential Guide

Need
– 2 –
Know

Johanna Payton

First published in Great Britain in 2009 by
Need2Know
Remus House
Coltsfoot Drive
Peterborough
PE2 9JX
Telephone 01733 898103
Fax 01733 313524
www.need2knowbooks.co.uk

Need2Know is an imprint of Forward Press Ltd.
www.forwardpress.co.uk

SB ISBN 978-1-86144-062-4
Cover photograph: Jupiter Images
Author photograph: Jane Stocks

Contents

Acknowledgements

This book wouldn't have been possible without the generous time and help of Martha Bishop, Penny Barber and Lisa Bartlett at Brook, Carolyn Phillips at Calthorpe Clinic and Lisa Hallgarten at Education for Choice. Thank you all.

Thanks also to Dr Sandra L. Wheatley, Dr Charlotte Zoltonos, Moira Wilson, Professor Hugh McLachlan, Ann Furedi at BPAS and the many interviewees who shared their personal experiences with me.

Special thanks to Matthew, EJ and my posse of extended family and friends for their enduring patience, input and support as I was writing, researching and talking ten to the dozen about the subject matter.

Introduction

A life-changing decision

Deciding to end a pregnancy may be a straightforward decision or one of the most difficult choices a woman has to make. However she feels, she needs support and information – but it's not always easy to ask for help or to reach the truth of the matter. Making choices without understanding all the facts, or going through abortion alone, can make it a more challenging and upsetting experience than it needs to be.

Abortion is a safe and common medical procedure used to end an unwanted pregnancy. According to Voice for Choice, the umbrella body for pro-choice organisations, one in three women has an abortion in her lifetime. Involving some emotional upheaval and soul-searching as well as the physical process, even when a woman has no doubt she wants to end a pregnancy, abortion is rarely undertaken lightly.

Many thousands of women decide whether or not to continue with a pregnancy each year. In 2007,198,500 women in England and Wales had an abortion.* Despite changing attitudes towards sex and morality, it's still a controversial and emotive subject many people have strong opinions about, or find hard to discuss.

The freedom to choose

There are many reasons women don't want to continue with a pregnancy. Although abortion is most common amongst women aged 18-24*, it can affect women of any reproductive age, their partners and families.

For some women, it's a lifestyle choice; they're not ready for a family. Others are still studying and feel too young to cope, particularly if they don't have a stable relationship. Women who already have children may make the decision based on financial or domestic situations, or they simply don't want any more children. Pregnancy can also pose a risk to a woman's health, or the foetus can have a serious or terminal health problem. Sadly, for some women, the fear of being sent abroad, made homeless, disowned by family or community, and even being killed, motivates their decision.

Every situation is different, but every woman is entitled to factual, supportive and non-judgemental advice. Having this information can help you make decisions that are best for your health, wellbeing and future.

* Figures released in June 2008 by the Department of Health.

Being prepared

Contemplating abortion is an incredibly personal choice. While no one can, or should, make it for you, getting to grips with the facts can help you make your decision. There's plenty of information out there about abortion, but not all of it is accurate or impartial. It's an issue clouded by emotion and surrounded in myth. Understanding it, however, is the key to making the best choice for you, and to supporting others.

If you're having an abortion, it's not unusual to feel daunted and scared. Asking questions at the clinic or hospital should be encouraged, but it's not always easy to quiz healthcare professionals. If you have an unwanted pregnancy, it's best to act quickly, but some women go through the procedure hurriedly, without understanding everything that's happened.

Counselling may (and should) be offered at some stage during the process as women who have the space to talk through their feelings are most likely to feel comfortable with their decision. If women find they are under-prepared for the way they feel at any stage, they may need additional support. They may just need to know that they're not alone.

Understanding abortion

Abortion – The Essential Guide is here to help you make choices and get through a challenging time. It will not make your decision for you; it simply presents the facts clearly and offers practical advice and support. It can also provide guidance for partners, parents and professionals.

In this non-judgemental book, you'll find everything you need to know about the different types of abortion, what the experience is like and how you might feel afterwards. If you're not sure whether or not you should have an abortion, reading this book should give you a good idea of how the entire process works, as well as looking at the alternatives, to help you make the decision that's right for you.

Women who've been through abortion talk frankly about their experiences so you don't have to fear the unknown. There is also professional advice to help you cope with what can be an emotional rollercoaster. If you've had an abortion, you'll find essential tips for a complete and successful recovery.

This may not be an easy time but with the facts to hand and plenty of support, you can come through it positively and move on with your life.

'The thing I'd do differently is get more information'

'I was 24 when I had my abortion. I'd only been with my partner for three months. He offered to support me through the pregnancy, but I was worried we'd never know if we'd stayed together because we loved each other or because we had a child.

'I didn't know anything about pregnancy or abortion. I got a leaflet but it didn't prepare me for my operation or the way I felt afterwards. I didn't want a baby but felt quite emotional. It was support from my partner and friends that speeded-up my recovery. Just talking to them made me feel better.

'If I could make the decision again, I'd still choose abortion. I stayed with my partner and we eventually married and had a baby. The thing I'd do differently is to get more information. I felt too intimidated to ask questions at the clinic and didn't read anything about the procedure. Being under-prepared made the experience scarier. I relied on other people but could have helped myself. If I'd been better prepared it would have been an easier experience.' Sharon, 34.

Disclaimer

Although this book has been written with the input and advice of medical professionals, it is primarily a collection of research and the author advises that she does not claim medical qualifications. Anyone who is contemplating an abortion, having treatment or recovering from the procedure should always consult their GP or healthcare professional for individual medical advice and reassurance. This book is for general information about abortion and is not intended to replace professional medical advice.

Names of all case studies have been changed.

Chapter One

An Unwanted Pregnancy

What are my options?

'Abortion was something I always said I wouldn't do, particularly after my first child. I got pregnant accidentally during a trial separation from my partner. I was on the pill but other medication I'd been taking interfered with it. I was back with my partner when I found out. He didn't know I'd had a fling and I didn't want him to.

'I sat for days contemplating what to do. I wanted another child – but not like this. I couldn't see any alternative to abortion. I wanted my relationship to work for the sake of my daughter, and how could I ask my partner to raise another man's child? Since having a termination I've had sleepless nights, wondering what could have been, but there would have been more hurt, pain and disaster if I'd gone through with the pregnancy.' Saida, 24.

If you're a woman of reproductive age and you have unprotected sex, even once, you could get pregnant. There are hundreds of myths about 'safe' positions, times of the month and even places in the house, but they are just that – myths.

You may have heard that you can't get pregnant while you're breastfeeding, on your period, before you've started your periods, after you've had an abortion or when you're on the pill – none of this is true.

Women will line up to tell you their stories of getting pregnant after they forgot to take their pill or before they'd started their periods (without realising they were about to start). Some women even get pregnant after sperm enters their vagina on fingers. Most methods of contraception are 99% safe when used properly – so an unlucky 1% of women with an active sex life will get pregnant in spite of contraception.

The most common indication of pregnancy is a missed period. Other early symptoms include:

- Sickness or nausea (not necessarily in the morning).
- Stomach cramps.
- Sore breasts.
- Using the toilet more often and/or being constipated.
- A strange, sometimes 'metallic' taste in your mouth.
- Feeling tired.
- Increased vaginal discharge.
- Light bleeding or 'spotting' which can be mistaken for a period.

If you think you might be pregnant, take a pregnancy test.

Taking a pregnancy test

Pregnancy tests work by detecting the hormone human chorionic gonadotrophin (hCG) which is in your urine during pregnancy. The test stick reacts when it comes into contact with hCG, so you hold the end of the stick in your urine flow and look for the result in the test window. Different test brands show the result in different ways (often using crosses or lines), so make sure you read the instructions.

Home pregnancy tests are sold in chemists, supermarkets, online and at health and beauty stores. If used properly, they're just as accurate as a doctor's test. Cost varies by brand, but tests from discount shops may not give accurate results. If you can't afford one, family planning clinics and young people's services, such as Brook, offer free tests. Most packs come with two tests inside.

Home pregnancy tests work from the first day of your missed period, but some sensitive tests can be used a day or two before. It is possible to have a false negative if you test too early or have an irregular menstrual cycle, so if your period hasn't started a week later, test again. A false positive result is very unlikely.

If you've only just had unprotected sex, the morning after pill can help you avoid unwanted pregnancy.

Emergency contraception

If you've just had unprotected sex or you think your contraception has failed, you can still take emergency contraception (the morning after pill) up to three days (72 hours) afterwards.

An emergency IUD (coil) can also be fitted up to five days after unprotected sex. Once fitted, you can keep it as a regular method of contraception.

Emergency contraception is free for all women, including under-16s. It's usually prescribed by a doctor but can sometimes be given by a nurse. You can access it via any GP (not just your own), a family planning clinic, a Brook centre and some pharmacies. You may have to pay if you go to a chemist.

For further information about the pill, see *The Pill – An Essential Guide* (Need2Know).

A positive pregnancy test

We've all seen the movies: two lines on the pregnancy test and the woman either jumps for joy or goes to pieces. The truth is, finding out you're pregnant triggers a range of emotions. Women who've been trying to get pregnant can still feel daunted and panicked by a positive result, while women who don't want a baby may be exhilarated at first.

However you feel, you can't ignore a positive pregnancy test.

If your pregnancy is unplanned, there are three possible outcomes:

- Becoming a parent.
- Continuing with the pregnancy and placing the baby for adoption.
- Terminating the pregnancy.

If your pregnancy was unplanned but you want a baby, make a doctor's appointment and take steps to ensure the pregnancy continues healthily, like eating well and not drinking or smoking.

Additional support from family, your partner and friends will also help. If you're struggling to break the news, ask for help and advice at a young person's clinic or talk to a counsellor. Professionals should always provide confidential and impartial help; you don't have to be alone.

Becoming a parent is a life-changing decision that needs to be made carefully. Having a baby can be a wonderful and fulfilling experience. It can also be expensive, stressful and demanding. Parenthood is rarely the answer to a problem – if you don't want a baby but someone is pressuring you to go through with a pregnancy, speak to someone who can provide professional advice.

'I imagined seeing those two pink lines and being thrilled. When I got pregnant unexpectedly at 19, to a boy who dumped me after sex, I was devastated.'

Claire, 20.

Should I have a baby?

If you're considering parenthood, it may help to write down how you feel about these questions:

- Why do I feel ready to be a parent or extend my family?
- How does my partner feel about becoming a parent?
- Have my friends and family agreed to help me and how?
- Why do I think I'm the right age to have a baby?
- How do I plan to raise a child properly?
- How might having a child help me achieve the things I want in life?
- Why do I want a child more than anything else?

Single parenting

If you're worried about going ahead with a pregnancy because you'll be a single parent, talk to friends and family to find out what kind of help they can offer. A strong network of support and the love of your extended family can be just as important and effective as a partner's.

Many agencies like Gingerbread (www.gingerbread.org.uk) can offer a good starting point for single parents, and parenting sites like www.netmums.com have online forums dedicated to single parents. If you're still at school or college and worried about dropping out of your education, talk to your teachers or tutors as they may have provisions in place to help you continue your education.

It can also help to talk to any single parents you know to find out how they cope and what help and support they have accessed. Meeting other people in the same boat as you and recognising that you're not alone can make all the difference.

An unwanted pregnancy

There are many reasons why a woman may not want to go through with a pregnancy. Some may include:

- She got pregnant accidentally or her contraception failed.
- No stable or long-term relationship.
- Feels the wrong age.
- Doesn't have enough money to support a child.
- Knows that a pregnancy will put her health at risk.
- There is a problem with the foetus.
- She became pregnant as a result of child abuse, sexual exploitation, rape or incest.
- Doesn't want any more children.
- Had a change in circumstances after planning pregnancy – such as separating from or losing her partner.
- Doesn't know who the father is or the pregnancy is the result of an affair.
- Fears the reaction of friends, family or community.

If you want to end a pregnancy and live in England, Wales or Scotland, you may be able to have an abortion. If you live in another country (including Northern Ireland and the Republic of Ireland where abortion is illegal), you can still access private abortion services in England, Wales or Scotland.

'I was shocked but excited when I found out. My boyfriend didn't feel the same. After talking it through, I realised he wasn't ready and I didn't want to be a single parent.'

Haley, 27.

Should I have an abortion?

If you're considering an abortion, it may help to write down how you feel about these questions:

- Will an abortion allow me to postpone becoming a parent or having more children until my situation is better?
- Will having a child now put my health, or the life that I want for myself, at risk?
- What do I want to achieve before I have a child?
- How does my partner feel about the pregnancy?
- Why am I afraid of becoming a single parent?
- Do I have someone to support me if I have an abortion?
- How will an abortion impact on my existing children?
- Am I worried about regretting an abortion later in life?
- What other options do I have available to me and how do I feel about them?

'Abortion is common and plays a part in many women's lives, yet, unlike other medical procedures, it is still stigmatised. We advocate the safe provision of abortion services and strive to normalise the treatment and its regulation.'

Ann Furedi, chief executive, British Pregnancy Advisory Service (BPAS).

Should I place the baby for adoption?

If you're considering adoption, it may help to write down how you feel about these questions:

- Do I want to postpone being a parent until a time when I feel ready?
- How would an abortion go against my personal beliefs?
- Why do I like the idea of giving my child to another family?
- How would I deal with giving the child to someone else after nine months of pregnancy and delivery?
- If I place the baby for adoption, how would I feel about someone else bringing up a child I gave birth to?
- Would my family support me if I placed the baby for adoption?
- Would I worry about the child contacting me when he/she is older?

Finding out your daughter is pregnant

Discovering your daughter's pregnancy can be a huge shock, however you feel later.

- Stay calm and avoid knee-jerk reactions.
- If you have strong feelings about abortion or pregnancy, be honest but take her feelings and opinions into account.
- Don't assume because you had an abortion or went ahead with an unplanned pregnancy that this is right for your daughter.
- If she's struggling to make a decision, help her gather information and go through it together.
- Be honest about the level of help and support you can give, whatever her decision.
- If she hasn't spoken to a healthcare professional, offer to go with her – but don't force her to take you.
- Encourage her to talk openly and honestly about her feelings.

Partner checklist

If your partner gets pregnant unexpectedly:

- Appreciate that her emotions and feelings might change as the news sinks in.
- Be honest, as well as tactful – don't promise anything you can't deliver. Don't just tell her what she wants to hear.
- If the pregnancy has knocked her confidence or self esteem, offer love and encouragement and assure her you'll respect her decision.
- She may need time and space – never rush her decision. Try to offer input without pressure. Ultimately, this is her choice.

Psychologist's view

'Women don't use abortion as a method of contraception. It takes strength and courage and certainly isn't a coward's way out. The women I work with often say it's a decision they will never feel good about but it was the right decision for them. These women had to admit that they weren't ready to have a child or to love and nurture it in the way it deserved. They acted with wisdom because they genuinely believed that having an unwanted child would be irresponsible.

'When a woman has an abortion because her pregnancy is the result of rape or abuse, she has already been victimised and needs as much support as possible so she can release the anger she's feeling. Women are very good at turning their anger inwards which can result in depression, so it's crucial they talk to someone in confidence for unconditional support.' Dr Sandra L. Wheatley PhD CPsychol, independent psychology consultant.

'Brook supports the provision of non-directive pregnancy counselling for women seeking information about their pregnancy choices and help with decision-making.'

Penny Barber, chief executive, Brook in Birmingham.

Getting help

You don't have to deal with an unwanted pregnancy alone. If you want help and support while making your decision, contact the following organisations:

- A local sexual health or contraceptive clinic (look in the phone directory or visit www.fpa.org.uk to find your nearest centre).
- A Brook centre (www.brook.org.uk).
- A teenage drop-in clinic or Connexions centre.
- Any independent, licensed abortion clinic.
- Your GP – to avoid delays it's worth asking if your GP has a moral objection to abortion before making an appointment.
- ChildLine (www.childline.org.uk or 0800 1111).
- Parentline Plus (www.parentlineplus.org.uk).
- British Association for Adoption and Fostering (www.baaf.org.uk).
- British Association for Counselling and Psychotherapy (www.bacp.co.uk) – ask for a counsellor who has no moral objection to abortion.

Summing Up

- If you experience an unplanned pregnancy, there are three options available.
- You can become a parent, place the baby for adoption or have an abortion.
- You can access support from a variety of sources to help you understand and consider your options.

Glossary

Contraception: any method used to stop a woman getting pregnant, including condoms, the pill and the coil.

Emergency contraception: a tablet that can be taken up to 72 hours after unprotected sex to prevent pregnancy.

Foetus: the medical name for a baby in the womb between the eighth week of pregnancy and the birth.

Menstrual cycle: the process (usually lasting three to five weeks) preparing your body for pregnancy each month, starting with the first day of your period and ending just before your next.

Reproductive age: the years during which you can have a baby, usually from when your periods start to the menopause.

Unprotected sex: having sex without contraception which can lead to pregnancy or catching a sexually transmitted infection (STI).

Chapter Two

What is an Abortion?

The end of a pregnancy

'When I found out I was 15 weeks pregnant, I was completely shocked. I was on the pill and had what I thought were periods, although they were light. I made my decision quickly because time was running out. I had no idea what an abortion involved and was terrified I'd have to go through labour. At the clinic they explained what a vacuum procedure entailed. Although it meant having a general anaesthetic, I was very relieved.' Kate, 24.

The definition of abortion

An abortion is a medical process ending a pregnancy so that it does not result in the birth of a baby. Healthcare professionals often refer to abortion as a 'termination of pregnancy' or 'termination'.

Abortion options depend on the stage of pregnancy. This is calculated by counting the number of weeks from the first day of your last period and is confirmed by an ultrasound scan.

The earlier the stage of pregnancy, the safer and more straightforward an abortion is, so it's important to seek advice quickly.

There are three main types of abortion:

- Early medical abortion (EMA) – up to nine weeks of pregnancy.
- Vacuum aspiration (also known as suction termination) – usually from seven to 15 weeks of pregnancy.

- Surgical dilation and evacuation (D&E) – usually from 15 to 24 weeks of pregnancy.

Other abortions:

- Medical abortion – from nine to 24 weeks of pregnancy.
- Abortions over 20 weeks of pregnancy (this may be D&E or medical induction) usually take place in a specialist clinic or hospital.

Miscarriage

Healthcare professionals sometimes refer to a miscarriage, where your body expels a pregnancy naturally, as a 'spontaneous abortion'. A miscarriage is different because the pregnancy ends without medical intervention.

If you have a miscarriage, which is common in early pregnancy, seek medical help. Treatment can't reverse a miscarriage once it's started, but even if you were unsure about continuing your pregnancy or were waiting for an abortion, it's important to prevent infection and check that your body has expelled all the pregnancy tissue.

Before an abortion

'Following an unexpected positive pregnancy test, some women choose to talk with a counsellor three or four times to enable them to make their decision. We're happy to see these women as often as they need to support them in making the right decision for them. If they decide not to continue with the pregnancy, the abortion methods available are discussed.' Martha Bishop, counselling manager, Brook in Birmingham.

Whether paying for a private abortion or going through the NHS, the process usually involves at least two appointments. The first is to discuss your situation and review treatment options, the second is to have the procedure itself. However:

- At some independent clinics it's possible to receive treatment on the same day you request it.
- Some clinics will complete an EMA over the course of a day.

At your first appointment you should have the opportunity to talk about your situation. If you feel confused or unsure, your healthcare professional should offer you time to consider your options, making an appointment for you to come back another day if necessary.

The decision to have an abortion is a matter between you and your healthcare team. The information and treatment you receive is confidential and can't be shared with anyone else without your agreement.

Although many women want to involve their partner, you have the right to choose an abortion without your partner's knowledge or agreement. Where men have tried to prevent abortions by taking legal action, they have failed.

At your first appointment you should:

- Have the opportunity to talk things through and to find out about counselling services.
- Be informed about the different methods of abortion and which one is suitable for your stage of pregnancy.
- Receive information about what to expect during and after the abortion.
- Be advised about any risks and complications related to the procedure.
- Find out where your abortion will take place – this could be at a local clinic. However, depending on your stage of pregnancy and where you live, you may need to travel.

'If you're unsure about continuing with the pregnancy, ask your GP or clinic about waiting times for abortions in your area. If you'll have to wait more than a few days, it makes sense to put your name on the list while you weigh up your options. You can change your mind right up until the last minute, but if you decide to have an abortion it can save valuable time.' Lisa Bartlett, programme development manager, Brook.

'At my first appointment I talked to the family planning nurse about contraception. The pill had let me down, so I had a coil fitted at the same time as the abortion.'

Abbey, 22.

The right procedure

To make sure the abortion you are offered is suitable for you, a doctor or nurse will ask questions about your medical history. They will also ask about your sexual history to check whether you should be tested for chlamydia or other sexually transmitted infections (STIs). If you have an abortion while carrying an STI it could cause a serious infection (see chapter 11), so a test is always advisable.

There are a number of procedures that take place before an abortion. These are routine, but if you have any concerns then make sure you talk to the doctor or nurse. They should explain why and if you need to have:

- A blood test.
- An ultrasound scan to confirm the stage of pregnancy and check the pregnancy isn't ectopic. The scan screen should be turned away. You can ask to see the scan images or have a print-out of the scan.
- Antibiotics to prevent infection after the abortion.
- Information, advice and agreement on which method of contraception to use afterwards. Increasing numbers of clinics offer to fit a long-lasting contraceptive at the same time as a surgical abortion. Alternatively, you may receive contraceptive pills or patches and condoms.
- Vaginal examinations (also known as 'internals'). These are now rare during early pregnancy.

Finally, you'll be given consent forms to sign. The rules of consent are different if you are under-16 (see chapter 5).

Questions to ask

At your first appointment it may be useful to ask:

- Will I need to take any time off work, school or college?
- How long will the procedure take?
- Will I visit the clinic more than once?
- Do I have to stay overnight?
- If I'm having an EMA in one day, can I leave the clinic in between taking the two drugs?
- Who will perform the procedure?

- Will I be offered counselling before or after my abortion?
- Can I bring someone with me to the clinic?
- Will my companion be able to stay with me all the time?
- Can I drive home afterwards?

Early medical abortion (EMA)

An EMA can be carried out up to nine weeks of pregnancy. You'll be given drugs that cause your body to reject the pregnancy in the same way as early miscarriage. You don't need anaesthetic or surgery and will be treated by a nurse rather than a doctor or surgeon.

Two different drugs work together to end the pregnancy. Some clinics ask you to come back one to three days after the first drug to take the second. Others will give you the second drug on the same day (six hours after the first).

The morning after pill (or emergency contraceptive pill) is not the same as an EMA. Rather than ending a pregnancy, the morning after pill stops you from getting pregnant.

You can read more about EMA in chapter 7.

'In 2007, 70% of abortions were carried out at under 10 weeks of gestation, with 90% carried out at under 13 weeks of gestation.'

Department of Health.

Vacuum aspiration abortion

Vacuum aspiration (or suction termination) is usually used from seven to 15 weeks of pregnancy and involves using gentle suction to remove the foetus from the womb.

The procedure usually takes between five and 10 minutes and can be carried out under a local or general anaesthetic.

It does not usually involve an overnight stay and requires only one visit to the clinic.

You can read more about a vacuum aspiration abortion in chapter 8.

Dilation and evacuation

Surgical dilation and evacuation (D&E) is carried out under general anaesthetic and may be used between 15 and 24 weeks of pregnancy. The cervix is gently stretched and dilated (opened) so that suction (and sometimes forceps, depending on the stage of the pregnancy) can be used to remove the foetus.

The procedure usually takes between 10-20 minutes. If you're healthy and there are no complications, you should be able to go home the same day.

You can read more about D&E in chapter 9.

Other abortion options

Most women who have an abortion will be offered one of the three main abortion methods. Other types of abortion are rare but may be performed in some circumstances. This largely depends on the stage of pregnancy, your general health and the method your clinic thinks is safest for you.

- You can read more about medical abortion in chapter 7.
- You can read more about late abortion (20 to 24 weeks) in chapter 9.

What happens after 24 weeks?

Abortion is legal in the UK up to 23 weeks and six days of pregnancy. There is no time limit if there is substantial risk to the woman's life or serious foetal abnormalities. The abortion time limit varies from country to country, but in the UK it is not possible to access an abortion if you discover you are pregnant during or after the 24th week.

If you are 24 weeks pregnant or over and do not want to become a parent, you can consider adoption:

- Contact the British Association for Adoption and Fostering (www.baaf.org.uk).
- Read more in *Adoption and Fostering – The Essential Guide* (Need2Know).

Reading more about abortion

Not all information you'll find about abortion is impartial.

Some anti-abortion (or 'pro-life') groups publish books and websites to influence women's decisions, claiming to offer information but actually trying to dissuade their readers from having abortions. There are also groups describing themselves as 'counselling services' which aim to prevent women from choosing abortion.

Groups opposed to abortion may try to influence a woman's decision using:

- Illustrations of foetuses or abortions taking place – an impartial group will never show you images unless you ask. The NHS *Pregnancy Book* includes accurate images of foetal development and is available to download from www.dh.gov.uk.
- Foetal images of late pregnancy, suggesting this is what early pregnancy looks like.
- Case studies of women who decided not to have abortions – other women's experiences are useful but your own circumstances and individual wishes are paramount.
- Overstated procedural risks and long-term mental and physical health problems – your healthcare provider can supply up-to-date statistics and information on any risks.
- Arguments against the use of contraception – many 'pro-life' groups are also opposed to contraception.

Although it is important to consider all your options, it is vital that the information you use to make your decision is balanced and never biased.

For more information on the 'pro-life' and 'pro-choice' debate, see chapter 5.

'At Calthorpe we work very hard in partnership with a woman, and within the law, to provide the service she wants whilst maintaining her dignity.'

Carolyn Phillips, manager, Calthorpe Clinic.

GP view

'Finding out you're pregnant when you were not planning to be can be a shock, and it's hard to deal with alone. Talking to your family doctor, a person you may have known for many years and who knows you extremely well, may offer you the support you need at a difficult time. At the surgery your GP and practice nurse should support you and talk about the options available. This will be confidential and will allow you to explore all possibilities. If you decide you want an abortion, the doctor or nurse can put you in touch with an organisation who can arrange this and provide support after the procedure. If you do not feel comfortable talking to a particular doctor or nurse, they should arrange for you to speak to another member of the team or put you in touch with someone that can help.' Dr Charlotte Zoltonos, GP.

'My GP booked a family planning clinic appointment on my behalf. It was posted in a plain NHS envelope addressed to me but marked confidential.'

Charley, 29.

Summing Up

- If you want to end a pregnancy, your GP or clinic should discuss all your options confidentially with you.
- There are three main types of abortion – which one you have depends on your stage of pregnancy.
- You can get as much information and advice as you need without any obligation to go through with an abortion.

Glossary

Anaesthetic: medicines used to temporarily reduce or take away sensation so that otherwise painful procedures or surgery can be performed.

Cervix: a narrow passage that leads from the womb to the vagina.

Ectopic pregnancy: when the egg gets fertilised anywhere other than the womb.

Miscarriage: when a pregnancy ends naturally before a foetus can survive outside the womb.

Ultrasound scan: a painless test that uses sound waves to create images of organs and structures inside your body.

Womb: also called a uterus, the womb is a pear-shaped organ in a woman's body where a foetus develops and grows.

Chapter Three

Having an Abortion

Acting quickly

'I didn't feel comfortable talking to my GP about a termination so I phoned BPAS. I was booked into a private clinic quickly and the vacuum aspiration procedure took place just before 12 weeks. The staff were considerate and non-judgemental and did all they could to make me feel comfortable. They accepted me as a human being going through a tough time rather than someone who should be burned at the stake for the decision I was making.' Rosa, 38.

The earlier in pregnancy a woman decides to have an abortion, the safer and more straightforward the procedure is. The sooner you seek advice, the less likely it is that you'll have to rush your decision, and you'll also have more treatment options.

Although the legal limit for abortion is 23 weeks and six days, it's easiest to access an NHS abortion before the 12th week of pregnancy. However, at any licensed clinic or hospital, abortions over 12 weeks are still safe and performed by fully-trained surgeons and anaesthetists.

Sometimes, the delay between a doctor's referral and the actual procedure can push you over the time limit for services in your local area. Travelling can add stress, as well as cost.

- If you're unsure about whether or not to continue with the pregnancy, and there is a waiting list in your area, you can always put your name down and withdraw it later.

'Travelling to access abortion services adds a huge burden, particularly for younger women. That's why the sooner you talk to a professional about your options, the more choice and flexibility you have.'

Lisa Hallgarten, head of policy and communication, Education for Choice.

- If you contact your nearest abortion clinic directly, they may be able to approach the Primary Care Trust (PCT) on your behalf so you can still access free NHS treatment.

If you're having an abortion before 12 weeks, you may be offered an early medical abortion (EMA) or a vacuum aspiration procedure. Pros and cons may include:

- You only need one appointment to have a vacuum aspiration and may experience less heavy bleeding at home.
- Some clinics offer a same day service for EMA, others ask you to attend two separate appointments one to three days apart.
- EMA is a nurse-led service, whereas surgical procedures are very likely to be performed by a male surgeon.
- The most effective method of abortion always depends on an individual and the stage of pregnancy.

'Department of Health figures for England, Wales and Scotland show that the total number of abortions in 2007 was 198,500 compared with 193,700 in 2006 – a rise of 2.5%.'

Who has an abortion?

Women of all ages and from all backgrounds have abortions for a wide and complex range of reasons. Although the majority of abortions take place before 12 weeks, women whose contraception failed without their knowledge may not realise they're pregnant until later. A University of Southampton paper ('Second-trimester abortions in England & Wales', April 2007) showed that over one in five under-16s who had abortions after 12 weeks didn't know that what they'd done could lead to pregnancy.

Although it isn't often or easily discussed, Voice for Choice (www.vfc.org.uk) reports that one in three women have an abortion in their lifetime, so it's likely someone you know has been through one. Hearing about their experiences may be helpful if you can confide in them.

Where to go for an abortion

There are two main routes if you want to have an abortion. If you live in England, Scotland or Wales, you may be able to access a procedure on the NHS or through a private clinic. Many private clinics provide abortion services for the NHS.

If you prefer to speak to a GP initially, they should explain what NHS and private abortion services are available locally.

- Abortions must be performed in an NHS hospital or clinic approved by the Department of Health.
- If you're worried about being recognised at a local clinic or hospital, ask about having the procedure elsewhere.

NHS abortions

If you want an NHS abortion, there are several options. You can contact:

- A local family planning clinic.
- Brook (if you're under 25).
- Any independent abortion clinic.
- Your GP.

To have an NHS abortion you need a referral from two doctors who agree that the requirements of the 1967 Abortion Act have been met (see chapter 5). If, for any reason, a healthcare professional cannot refer you for an NHS abortion, they should help you find someone who can.

If you see your GP first, you'll normally be referred for a consultation at a local hospital or clinic to confirm the stage of your pregnancy, consider treatment options and arrange an appointment for your abortion. The consultation should usually be offered within a week. If you go to a family planning clinic, Brook or an independent clinic, they can refer women for abortion services through the NHS in the same way GPs do.

You don't have to pay for an NHS abortion but NHS services do depend on where you live.

- According to www.nhs.uk, NHS abortion provision ranges from over 90% of local demand to less than 60%, according to the area.
- A survey by Voice for Choice found that the percentage of abortions performed or funded by the NHS in England in 2002 varied between PCTs from 46% to 96%.
- In some areas the NHS will pay for abortions in private clinics.

Some NHS hospitals and clinics will only do abortions up to 12 weeks, unless there are exceptional circumstances. If your local hospital won't accept you, ask for information about other hospitals or clinics in the area or further afield.

'Department of Health figures for England, Wales and Scotland show that 89% of abortions in 2007 were funded by the NHS – 57% took place in the independent sector under NHS contract.'

- If you live outside England, Scotland or Wales, you are not entitled to an NHS abortion but should still be able to access private treatment, providing you're less than 24 weeks pregnant.
- Abortion law in England, Scotland and Wales does not extend to Northern Ireland. Women there don't have access to NHS abortion services. Different laws also apply in Jersey, Guernsey and the Isle of Man (see chapter 5).

My NHS abortion

'My GP had a moral issue with abortion but booked me in to see another doctor later that day. I'm glad it was a woman because it was easier to talk about my situation. She referred me and 10 days later I had an appointment at a local clinic where I was given an ultrasound to confirm my dates. They asked about my medical history, explained how medical abortion worked and gave me a tablet to take before making an appointment to go back 36 hours later for a pessary. I had a follow-up appointment three weeks later to check everything was okay.' Sarah, 24.

Private abortions

If you visit a private clinic, you can arrange an appointment without a referral from your GP. Some private clinics can treat you and receive NHS funding for the service, so it's worth asking about your options.

At a private clinic the procedure is similar to the NHS:

- The agreement of two doctors is needed.
- You can talk to a nurse or counsellor if you want to discuss your situation.
- You'll have a medical check, any necessary tests, a scan to determine how many weeks pregnant you are and time to talk about treatment options.
- The abortion may take place on the same day as your consultation or arranged for another day.

A private abortion may save you time if you live in an area with long NHS waiting times, but you will have to pay. Costs at private clinics vary but usually depend on:

- Stage of pregnancy (earlier abortions may be less expensive).
- Method of abortion used.
- Which organisation carries out the abortion.

Early abortions start from around £350 and go up to £750 or above after 12 weeks.

- Some private clinics offer repayment schemes so you don't have to pay for the procedure in one lump sum.
- The Healthcare Commission (www.healthcarecommission.org.uk) publishes reports on approved abortion clinics, based on annual inspections. You can access these reports online.

'Calthorpe is the biggest independent abortion clinic in the country and 90% of the procedures that take place here are funded by the NHS.'

Carolyn Phillips, manager, Calthorpe Clinic.

My private abortion

'I'm from Dublin, where abortion is illegal. I didn't want to continue my pregnancy; I was in the middle of studying and felt too young to be a mum. I knew an abortion in England would be expensive, but it was cheaper than raising a baby. I found a clinic on the Internet, arranged an appointment for the following week and booked a flight, bringing my sister for support. The ultrasound showed I was further along in the pregnancy than I thought. The staff put me at ease, arranging a surgical abortion for the next day. Although the procedure was uncomfortable, everything was explained and I felt fine a couple of hours after leaving theatre. I was discharged the same afternoon.' Gillian, 21.

Delays

Whether you seek a private or NHS abortion, you should be given help and advice as quickly as possible, even if there is a waiting list for the procedure.

If you feel the process is being unduly held up (waiting for pregnancy test results, being told it's too late when you're under 24 weeks, being told to think about it after you've made your decision, etc.), contact an advisory centre like Brook or BPAS.

Confidential treatment

An abortion is between you and your healthcare provider. All information is confidential, regardless of your age and whether you have private or NHS treatment. This means that information cannot be shared with anyone else without your agreement. The clinic is also not required to tell your GP where you are having your abortion.

- If you're treated at an independent clinic, you'll be given a unique reference number. If the clinic needs to invoice the local PCT for the service it has provided, it refers to you by using the number and not your name.
- Many abortion services like to let your GP know about an abortion in case of complications and so your medical records can be updated. They can only do this with your permission. Tell the clinic if you don't want them to inform your GP.
- Although you might not want your GP to know about an abortion right now, you might want to consider it later, particularly if you go ahead with a future pregnancy. Having all your medical information will help a GP provide the very best treatment.
- If a GP is obstructive or refuses to advise you on moral grounds, you may want to use a different doctor in the future. You are entitled to change your GP at any time without giving a reason. Speak to the receptionist at your practice or contact your local health authority to move to another surgery entirely.
- If you want to complain about any treatment or advice you have received, contact the Healthcare Commission (www.healthcarecommission.org.uk).

Support checklist

If you're supporting a woman having an abortion:

- Be honest about any reservations you have – if you don't feel able to support her, help find someone who can.
- Offer to attend clinic appointments, but be patient and understanding. All clinics will want to see her for at least some time alone to check she is happy with her decision. You may also be asked to leave during treatment.
- Read information she's given so you understand the process too.
- If you need additional support, don't hesitate to tell the clinic or hospital. They should offer you information on local support groups or agencies.

Improved services?

'Some women still experience delays in being referred for an abortion when health professionals do not declare a conscientious objection, or they face long waiting times for a hospital appointment. Additional delay increases the distress of women experiencing an unwanted pregnancy. Access to sexual health services is improving, but much more work is needed. Women should certainly not be exposed to any additional and unnecessary delays in the referral process.' Penny Barber, chief executive, Brook in Birmingham.

Changing your mind

You can change your mind about an abortion right up until the moment the procedure starts.

- Staff at clinics and hospitals will always understand.
- They appreciate a phone call to cancel any appointments you've made.
- If you were planning a private abortion and change your mind, you may be charged for a consultation but will not have to pay for the procedure.

- Women are encouraged to complete a medical abortion once they have started the procedure – the first tablet, mifepristone, may cause the abortion on its own.

Becoming a parent

If you decide to continue with the pregnancy, it's helpful to talk to those closest to you, finding out what level of support they can offer.

Further sources of help:

- A local GP will book you in for antenatal appointments with midwives. They will provide healthcare, answer questions and give you information about local support services and classes.
- Visit the NHS online Pregnancy Care Planner at www.nhs.uk/planners/pregnancycareplanner.
- Net Doctor (www.netdoctor.co.uk) has a large section on pregnancy and birth.
- tiger.direct.gov.uk/cgi-bin/maternity.cgi and www.dwp.gov.uk/advisers/ni17a/ contain information about maternity pay and benefits.
- www.babycentre.co.uk and www.netmums.com have information and communities of expectant and new parents.
- Single parents can access support from www.gingerbread.org.uk and *Single Parents – The Essential Guide* (Need2Know).
- Mother 35 Plus (www.mothers35plus.co.uk).
- *Teenage Pregnancy – The Essential Guide* (Need2Know).

Adoption

If you decide to go ahead with the pregnancy but place the baby for adoption, start your journey by contacting the British Association for Adoption and Fostering (www.baaf.org.uk). You can also read *Adoption and Fostering – The Essential Guide* (Need2Know) for further information.

Summing Up

- It's important to act quickly if you want access to an abortion.
- You may be able to access a free NHS abortion, or pay for one at a private clinic.
- You should receive help and information without delay and can complain if you are obstructed.
- You can change your mind right up until the last minute.

Glossary

Antenatal care: the treatment you receive during a continuing pregnancy.

Foetal abnormality: A serious health or developmental problem with a foetus.

NHS: the National Health Service.

Midwife: specialist healthcare providers for pregnant women and new mothers.

Chapter Four
Making a Decision

Your choice

'I planned to get pregnant; I suspected my boyfriend was going to finish with me so I stopped taking my pill. He was angry and didn't want anything to do with the pregnancy. I hadn't thought through becoming a parent and the reality hit me like a ton of bricks.

'Luckily, my best friend helped me decide and we talked to her sister, who'd had a termination. I weighed up the pros and cons, but my main fear was becoming a single parent. I decided to have an abortion and believe it was the best choice.' Christine, 21.

Whether or not to continue with a pregnancy is an important decision. When you're making up your mind, accessing information on all your options is essential.

Pretending the pregnancy isn't happening or leaving your decision to the last minute could limit your options, so it's best to get help and start the decision-making process as soon as you can.

A straightforward solution

For some women, deciding to have an abortion is straightforward and doesn't involve a great deal of deliberation.

There's nothing to say it must be a difficult decision. Although it's wise to consider all your options so you can look back on your decision with confidence and assurance, it's perfectly normal to make your choice with complete certainty.

If this is the case, don't beat yourself up – it doesn't mean you're uncaring or unfeeling. Lots of women with unplanned pregnancies know immediately that they don't want to, or cannot, continue. Whether you make a decision within hours or days, making an informed choice will help you recover fully and move on.

A difficult decision

'My partner wanted me to keep the baby, but he was still taking drugs. It wouldn't have been any life for me or a child. We split up over it, but I was glad the pregnancy brought things to a head.'

Kelly, 19.

'We provide abortion services for 60,000 women each year but counsel larger numbers, many of whom decide to continue with an unplanned pregnancy. Our research has shown that the decision-making process can be incredibly long and difficult for some. However long it takes, we recognise that women can be trusted to make their own decision; even if it turns out to be the wrong choice, it is theirs to make.' Ann Furedi, chief executive, BPAS.

The decision to have an abortion can be particularly difficult for a wide and complex range of reasons, including:

- You want to be a mother, just not right now.
- You want to continue with the pregnancy but your partner or family doesn't (or vice versa).
- Your religious, social or cultural upbringing has encouraged you to oppose abortion, or shuns single parents.
- You already have children and weren't planning to extend your family.
- You're not sure if you can afford a baby.
- Your pregnancy was planned but your circumstances have changed.
- You've been told that there's a problem with the foetus.
- You've been told that continuing with the pregnancy will put your health at risk.

Although they may want to end a pregnancy, many women are wary of abortion because they are worried about what people will think of them and scared that it will hurt or damage their fertility. Many women feel abortion is something that would never happen to them.

If you're struggling with your decision, it can help to talk to someone who can be objective and impartial, like a professional counsellor or health worker. Family and friends may want to support you but can't help having a vested interest in the outcome of your decision. Knowing how they feel can play a crucial part in your decision-making, but it must be your decision.

Feeling confused

There are lots of reasons for feeling confused. Even in early pregnancy you can experience mood swings, so your emotions might feel heightened because of the physical changes happening to your body. Stress can also intensify your emotions; for most women, an unplanned pregnancy is very stressful.

- How you feel about the pregnancy could change by the day or hour. It might seem like a great idea one minute and a disaster the next.
- It helps to list your emotions as you experience them.
- In times when you're feeling less emotional and more clear-headed, look at your situation objectively to see if you feel more strongly one way or the other.

Other people's opinions can confuse your decision-making process. They may tell you what is right or wrong. They might become excited about the prospect of you continuing with the pregnancy, or they might say you would be crazy to go ahead.

- Others won't be dealing with the consequences of your decision in the same way as you – what's right for them isn't necessarily in your best interests.
- If your partner is pressuring you either way, go through the pros and cons together – being honest about how you both feel will help you make a decision.

Weighing up pros and cons

There are practical strategies you can employ to help make your decision.

- Consider your three main options and fill in the following statements:

- The idea of having a baby makes me feel.....because...
  - The idea of placing a baby for adoption makes me feel...because...
  - The idea of having an abortion makes me feel...because...
- Write a list of pros and cons for each available option – comparing the lists helps you see which option may be best for you.
- Although you can't predict the future, it may help to list any potential consequences attached to your options. Ask yourself where you might be in one, five or 10 year(s) if:
  - You become a parent.
  - You place a baby for adoption.
  - You have an abortion.

You can't be certain what the consequences of your choice will be, but carefully considering your future helps you to see which option is likely to have the best outcome.

- Write down the names of the important people in your life and think about how your decision will impact on them. Consider finding out if they really feel that way rather than making a decision based on presumptions.
- Keep a diary of your feelings as you come to your decision – as well as helping you decide, it will be useful to look back at in the months and years ahead, reminding you why you made the choice you did.
- It's natural to feel that whatever decision you make isn't 'perfect' – an unplanned pregnancy is rarely a perfect scenario for any woman. You may continue to have mixed feelings, but ask yourself if you can cope with them; if you can, it could be time to act on your decision.

Getting support

Impartial help

'Talking to someone who isn't emotionally related to the situation can be helpful. As counsellors, we offer unbiased support to help clients make an empowered decision. We check where they are in their decision-making process and how they feel about it. We welcome supportive partners, parents or friends but always give women an opportunity to see us on their own, even for a short time, so they can talk in complete confidence. We're here to support women whatever they choose to do and give them enough time and space to look at the best options for them.' Martha Bishop, counselling manager, Brook in Birmingham.

If you want to find a counsellor, ask your GP or clinic for a local list. Contact the following organisations to find a counsellor independently:

- British Association for Counselling and Psychotherapy (www.bacp.co.uk).
- Counselling Directory (www.counselling-directory.org.uk).

Counsellors won't make your decision for you or tell you what to do, but they can help you explore your options and work out the best way forward. Like GPs, some counsellors have conscientious objections to abortion. Check before you make an appointment and be aware that some anti-abortion groups offer 'pregnancy counselling' designed to influence a woman's decision.

'I didn't think the nurses or doctors were very friendly at the clinic, but the short counselling session was lovely. The counsellor helped me to see I had nothing to feel guilty or ashamed of.'

Nyla, 27.

A partner's role

'For some men, the decision around an unplanned pregnancy may be straightforward; if that's how his partner feels too, they can support each other through the process. If they differ, the man can feel angry, sad, scared or helpless – and the decision can affect him for the rest of his life. It is important for him to talk about his thoughts and feelings and think about the possible consequences.' Martha Bishop, counselling manager, Brook in Birmingham.

Keeping a secret

If you decide to continue with the pregnancy, you might keep it secret until you've plucked up the courage to talk to your parents or partner, particularly if you don't want them to know you've been sexually active.

Even if you're not ready to share, seek good medical care and advice as soon as possible. Talking confidentially to a professional who can provide information and advice for a healthy pregnancy is crucial.

You don't have to tell anyone about deciding to have an abortion, but it may help to talk to someone you trust. If you decide to confide in friends, ask yourself:

- Can you trust them to keep the information to themselves?
- Do they have strong opinions?
- Will they provide a listening ear rather than trying to give you advice?
- Are they a reliable source of support and comfort?

Breaking the ice

If you want to ask parents/carers, your partner, family members or friends for support:

- Choose an appropriate time and place.
- Use what you know about their beliefs and opinions to prepare for their reaction, but expect the unexpected – people feel differently about issues when they happen to someone they care about.
- If you're sharing two major pieces of information (admitting that you've had sex, as well as telling someone you're pregnant), this may trigger a dramatic or emotional initial response. If you're worried that they will fly off the handle, consider having someone impartial there to keep the peace.
- Don't assume their immediate reaction represents their real feelings – they may be shocked, angry, upset or even silent, yet their standpoint may change with time.

- If you've already confided in someone and you're building-up to telling another, use role play to practise the conversation you're going to have.
- Hypothetical situations are different to real ones; if you ask your mum what she thinks about abortion in general, for example, her answer won't reflect the way she feels about you having the procedure.
- Keep any information about your options to hand.
- If you've already made your decision, writing down your reasons and going through them together can be really helpful – they can see you're making a considered choice.
- Remember that the person you're telling may have either gone through an abortion or been close to someone who has.
- If your decision is against the wishes of your family or partner and you feel distressed or at risk of harm, contact someone who can help:
  - ChildLine (0800 1111 / www.childline.org.uk).
  - Connexions (www.connexions-direct.com).
  - Relate (www.relate.org.uk).
  - National Domestic Violence Helpline (0808 2000 247 / www.nationaldomesticviolencehelpline.org.uk)

'Many women arrive at the clinic having already made their decision with support from their partner, friends and families. They don't have to tell us how they came to that decision.'

Carolyn Phillips, manager, Calthorpe Clinic.

Will I regret an abortion?

No one can answer that question.

Rather than regretting the abortion, many women say they regret getting pregnant in the first place. However, if you've made an independent and informed choice, you're much less likely to regret it.

Women are less likely to say they regret having a child once it's been born, but that doesn't mean they don't have regrets. They may regret sacrifices they made, missed opportunities or relationships that failed or changed once they became parents.

Like all important decisions, you may look back with a mixture of emotions and feel differently at various points in life. It helps to know that at the time you made your decision, it was for the right reasons.

Supporting her decision-making

'Parents get incredibly frustrated when their daughter makes a decision that they don't think is right, but they should only offer their opinions and respect her right to make the choice that's right for her.'

Lisa Bartlett, programme development manager, Brook.

A woman experiencing an unplanned pregnancy may find it extremely difficult to ask for help, so if you're a partner, parent or professional, use this checklist to ensure you give the best possible support you can:

- Often, the first person a woman talks to is the one she trusts most, so even if you're not confident enough to deal with the situation yourself, offer to support her as she seeks further advice and information.
- Assure her that your conversation will be treated in confidence. Respect that confidentiality.
- If you're a professional, aim to offer the woman a safe space in which she can discuss her feelings and identify her hopes, fears, needs and desires. Use non-judgemental listening skills and appropriate boundaries.
- Ask her why she thinks she might be pregnant in case she can still take emergency contraception.
- Agree on a realistic timeframe for decision-making, taking the stage of pregnancy into account.
- Ask whether she knows there are three available options: parenthood, adoption or abortion.
- If you're a parent or partner, talk about the impact each option will have on you both and how your circumstances will change. Be honest about the support you'll give – don't make false promises.
- No matter what you know about her religious, cultural and social background, don't presume what her decisions about pregnancy will be – listen and keep an open mind.
- Help her explore all available options, using evidence-based information.
- Find sources of support outside her family or community if she's being pressured into making a decision either way.

- Although it's tempting to offer answers to 'what should I do?' or 'what would you do if you were me?', keep the discussion focused on her situation and options.
- If you have strong personal opinions about pregnancy, adoption or abortion, and don't feel you can offer impartial support, resist pressing your beliefs onto her. Help her find alternative, impartial support instead.

Making a decision after a scan

If you're forced to make a decision after a routine scan detects a foetal abnormality, or because the pregnancy is threatening your health, you may need specialist help and support.

Antenatal Results and Choices (www.arc-uk.org) provides non-directive support and information to expectant and bereaved parents throughout and after the antenatal screening and testing process.

Summing Up

- When deciding whether or not to continue with a pregnancy, every woman will have a different set of pros and cons to weigh up.
- Help and support from others can help your decision-making. However, if others have strong opinions, they can make it more difficult for you.
- You're less likely to regret your decision if you make an independent and informed choice.

Glossary

Conscientious objector: an individual who refuses to participate in something on religious, moral or ethical grounds.

Counsellor: a qualified professional who sees a client, at their request, in a private and confidential setting to explore a difficulty the client is having and their feelings.

Foetal abnormality: a serious health or developmental problem with a foetus.

Chapter Five

Abortion, Ethics, Religion and the Law

Right or wrong?

'I was raised in the Catholic faith and taught to oppose abortion – I fell out with a friend at school when she had one. When I got pregnant accidentally after a one night stand, I'd just started university. I didn't want to end a life and I knew my parents would try to persuade me to have a baby, but if I had to put my studies and career on hold to have a child, I knew I'd resent it. Bringing a baby into the world that I didn't want seemed more sinful than having an abortion.' Jackie, 23.

Although abortion is a safe procedure that can be carried out legally in England, Scotland and Wales under 24 weeks, the provision of pregnancy termination services continues to be a controversial, emotive and widely-debated subject.

The abortion debate is centred on:

- Whether it is ever morally acceptable to terminate a pregnancy.
- Whether abortion should be legal or illegal.

Abortion is a subject provoking strong views. Although many people have a flexible approach and believe every situation is individual, some people, describing themselves as 'pro-life', think abortion is always wrong. Others, who may call themselves 'pro-choice', believe there are a range of circumstances

'Sometimes what appears to be a problem or a question is actually a dilemma. Dilemmas have no solutions and no answers. With dilemmas, we must try to choose the least uncomfortable available option.'

Professor Hugh McLachlan, School of Law and Social Sciences, Glasgow Caledonian University.

in which abortion is morally acceptable and women should have the right to an abortion if they want one. Abortion Rights (www.abortionrights.org.uk) reports that 76% of the UK population is pro-choice.

A complex argument

The ethics of abortion, however, are much more complex than a 'for or against' debate. Some people may personally feel that abortion is immoral but also believe in individual choice and think that it shouldn't be outlawed. They may believe that having an unwanted child, or continuing with a pregnancy when the mother's health or the health of the foetus is compromised, is not always the best option for a woman or society as a whole.

Even when people agree that abortion is morally acceptable, they don't think it is the best course of action in every situation where a pregnancy is unplanned.

Although they agree about the right to choose abortion, pro-choice supporters may disagree about the point at which abortion becomes unethical or untenable – some would prefer to see the 24 week limit extended, others would like to see it reduced and some think it is best left as it is.

People also have varying opinions about when a life becomes a life and whether a foetus is actually a human being or part of a woman's body. Even among people who believe that a foetus is a person, there's no clear agreement about the rights an unborn and undeveloped person has, or should have.

Some people believe that the issue of foetal viability is key to the debate. Due to developments in neo-natal care, babies born from 24 weeks of gestation have an improving chance of survival. There is also a perception that a foetus has a better chance of survival before 24 weeks. The world's most premature baby was delivered in the US at just under 22 weeks – but such cases are extremely rare.

Medical organisations including the British Medical Association, the Royal College of Nursing and the Royal College of Obstetricians and Gynaecologists agree there is no evidence of significant improvement in pre-term infant survival below 24 weeks. Department of Health figures for 2007 also show that 90% of abortions in the UK took place prior to 13 weeks of gestation, long before a foetus could survive outside the womb.

It's rare to find anyone who thinks that abortion is 'great'. Pro-choice people don't advocate abortion as a form of birth control; they campaign for the continued provision of legal abortion services because there is no 100% effective contraceptive method. Most people agree that abortion is a last resort and, although accidents happen, it's much better to avoid an unwanted pregnancy wherever possible.

'I didn't plan either of my pregnancies and I'm a single parent. I couldn't go through with an abortion because I was brought up to believe that life begins when you've conceived. I'd find it too hard to live with the guilt if I ended a life.'

Faiza, 23.

Abortion and the law

'People assume we have liberal abortion laws in the UK, but women don't have an automatic legal right to an abortion. They need the consent of two doctors who must agree that a woman meets a certain criteria to be referred for an abortion. If doctors applied this criteria to the letter, far fewer abortions would take place. I'd like to see a change in the law giving women greater access to abortion so a doctor is not required to interpret the law in his or her own way.' Professor Hugh McLachlan, School of Law and Social Sciences, Glasgow Caledonian University.

According to the 1967 Abortion Act (which originally legalised the provision of abortion up to the 28th week of pregnancy) and the Human Fertilisation and Embryology Act 1990 (which amended the 1967 law), an abortion in England, Scotland and Wales is legal up to 24 weeks of pregnancy when two registered medical practitioners agree that it is necessary because:

- Continuing with the pregnancy would harm the woman's mental or physical health more than having the abortion, or
- Continuing with the pregnancy would harm the mental or physical health of any children she already has.

These criteria are broad and most doctors ask a woman to explain how she feels about the pregnancy before using their own judgement. Many believe that a woman is the best person to make a decision about her pregnancy, referring any patient who requests an abortion on the grounds that her mental health will suffer by being forced to continue with a pregnancy she doesn't want.

Doctors may also assess the situation on the basis that abortion is statistically safer than carrying a pregnancy to term and giving birth. Therefore, following this argument, abortion always represents a lesser threat to a woman's health than pregnancy, so any woman requesting an abortion should have one on health grounds.

There is no time limit when two doctors agree that a woman's health or life is gravely threatened by continuing with a pregnancy, or that the foetus is likely to be born with severe physical or mental abnormalities. If an abortion must be performed as a matter of medical emergency, a second doctor's agreement is not necessary.

'In 2007, the under-16 abortion rate was 4.4 per 1,000 women. The abortion rate was highest at 36 per 1,000 for women aged 19. The under-18 rate was 19.8 per 1,000 women.'

Department of Health figures, 2007.

The 1967 Abortion Act also states that a legally induced abortion must be performed by a registered medical practitioner in an NHS hospital, or other location approved for the purpose of the act.

Before the 1967 Abortion Act, abortion was illegal in England, Scotland and Wales, except to save the life of the pregnant woman. Abortions were still performed illegally but there were greater risks of complications.

Conscientious objectors

As in wider society, some doctors think abortion is always wrong. These doctors are within their rights not to refer a woman for abortion on the grounds of their own conscientious objection.

- Government guidance says that women should not be prevented from seeing a doctor who may refer them for abortion in the event their own doctor refuses.
- If a doctor has a personal objection to abortion, he or she should make this clear and offer to arrange an appointment with another doctor for you.
- If a doctor is obstructive or tries to influence your decision, you have the right to see another professional.

Can women under 16 have an abortion?

The age of consent for medical treatment, including abortion, is 16. However:

- The law says a girl under 16 can consent to her own treatment without her parents' or carers' permission if two doctors believe it's in her best interests and she's mature enough to make her decision independently, understanding what is involved.
- Health workers use guidelines called 'The Fraser Guidelines' to assess whether a young person is mature enough to make their own decision and if it is in their best interests.
- Even if a woman is under 16, doctors and other health workers must keep what is said private. Even if they don't think she's mature enough to consent, they should not share any information about her request for treatment unless they believe her safety, or that of another, is at risk. If they're thinking of talking to another professional or agency, they normally talk to the woman first.
- You can ring a service anonymously to ask about their policy for protecting young people and whether they see under-16s in confidence.
- Doctors will offer support and advice, and should help young women to explore the benefits of talking to a parent or carer.
- Support and care from parents can help young women recover and deal with the practicalities of an abortion, like travelling to the clinic and taking time off school to recover.
- Clinic workers say it's very rare for under-16s not to have any parental support or involvement.

Having an abortion under 16

'I didn't want to tell Dad I was pregnant because I was 15, but the clinic nurse said he might understand and support me. She wanted my dad to sign some forms too. Dad shouted at first – he was more upset about me having sex than being pregnant. When he calmed down, he helped me decide what to do. We went to the clinic together. I felt proud not to be on my own. Dad waited all day and I was glad to see him after the operation. I'm pleased my abortion isn't a secret.' Gabrielle, 16.

If you're worried about telling parents or carers:

- If you don't think you can tell a parent or carer, ask yourself if there's another meaningful adult in your life who can help – older brothers or sisters, a friend's mum or a teacher, for example.
- An organisation like Brook or the FPA will help as best they can. They may even offer to come with you when you tell your parents, or help you find a way to ask for their support.
- If you think telling a parent or carer will put you at risk of harm, contact ChildLine (www.childline.org.uk) for help.

Abortion laws outside England, Scotland and Wales

'According to Department of Health figures, 7,100 abortions for non-residents were carried out in hospitals and clinics in England and Wales during 2007.'

- The 1967 Abortion Act does not extend to Northern Ireland where abortion is against the law (apart from in very extreme circumstances). Most women who want abortions travel to England, Wales or Scotland and arrange private treatment through organisations like Marie Stopes, Calthorpe Clinic or BPAS. They cannot access NHS services.
- Abortion is also illegal in the Republic of Ireland, although the law allows pregnant women to receive counselling and information about their options and does not prevent women travelling abroad for a termination. Some anti-abortion groups pose as counselling services in Ireland.
- In Jersey, according to the Termination of Pregnancy (Jersey) Law 1997, abortion is legal as long as the woman is no more than 12 weeks pregnant. Between 12 and 24 weeks it's permitted only in extreme circumstances. A similar law exists in Guernsey.
- In the Isle of Man, the Termination of Pregnancy Act 1995 states that abortions can only be legally performed under extreme conditions. Although abortions can be obtained via a legal process, it can be lengthy. As a result, most women travel abroad for private treatment.

Abortion around the world

- Abortion laws vary from country to country; in Malta the procedure is banned entirely, whereas in Canada there are no restrictions on the provision of abortion.

- National abortion laws do not always reflect the religion of the country.

Legal advice

For more information about abortion and your legal rights, contact:

- Brook (www.brook.org.uk).
- www.thesite.org.
- Community Legal Advice (www.communitylegaladvice.org.uk).

Abortion and religion

Most religions take a strong position on abortion and no religion actively supports it. Although a few religions oppose abortion under all circumstances, some accept that there are situations when abortion may be necessary.

Religions are interested in abortion because they believe the issue encompasses profound issues of life and death, right and wrong and human relationships. They may also view abortion and our attitudes towards it as symbolic of society as a whole.

- While some religions view abortion as morally wrong, they don't necessarily think it should be punishable.
- When making decisions about pregnancy and abortion, people of faith usually try to balance their own circumstances with the teachings of their religion.
- You can read more about abortion and religion by downloading a factsheet at www.efc.org.uk/Foryoungpeople/Factsaboutabortion/Religion.

A man's legal rights

'In the UK, a man has no legal rights over abortion. All legal challenges by men trying to prevent a partner having an abortion have failed to date. The law dictates that the decision to terminate a pregnancy is made by a woman and approved by two doctors. However, if a woman wants to make a truly informed choice about whether or not to continue with pregnancy, knowing how her partner feels could be part of the information she needs to make her decision. Whatever that decision is, she might get more support from her partner if she gives him the opportunity to express his feelings and listen to hers. This may also benefit the relationship in the long-term.' Lisa Hallgarten, head of policy and communication, Education for Choice.

- Agencies like Brook provide an opportunity for young men to talk about their feelings, with or without their partner. Men over 25 can access support through counselling or their GP.

Summing Up

- The abortion debate involves ethics, religion, social responsibility and the law, but it is important to separate these factors.
- Whatever values your faith and upbringing have instilled in you, it is likely that your choices will also be informed by your unique situation and personal aspirations.

Glossary

Consent: give acceptance or approval on a course of action.

Ethical: dealing with morals or rights and wrongs.

Foetal viability: the ability of a foetus to survive after birth.

Gestation: the time a foetus has spent in the womb.

Moral: a code of conduct in matters of right and wrong.

Neo natal care: special care for sick or pre-term babies.

Pre-term or premature baby: a baby born before the 37th week of pregnancy.

Chapter Six

Preparing for Abortion

Before you go ahead with an abortion, use these checklists to help you prepare.

Questions to ask your healthcare provider

- Can you provide a letter for my school or employer so I can take time off?
- How do I get to the clinic?
- What happens if I'm late for my appointment?
- Can I park in a private car park?
- Do I need to bring any referral letters or other details with me?
- Will I need to fill forms in on the day of my treatment?
- Do I still have to give the name of my next of kin, even if they don't know about my abortion?
- Do I have to provide my GP's details?
- What's the schedule for the day when I arrive for my treatment?
- Do I need to have a full bladder for the scan?
- Will I be treated by male members of staff?
- When do I pay the fee?
- Who can I bring with me?
- Can my companion stay with me?
- Is there a crèche or childcare facility at the clinic?

- Can I take my prescription medication as normal on the day of treatment?
- Can I take any other drugs before my treatment?
- If I'm taking methadone, can I take it on the day of my treatment?
- Can I eat and drink before the procedure?
- Can I smoke before or during the treatment?
- Can I use my mobile phone in the clinic?
- Can I wear jewellery and/or make-up during the treatment?
- Do I need to bring my own sanitary towels?
- What kind of sanitary towels should I bring?
- Can I buy sanitary towels at the clinic?
- Will I wear a hospital gown or can I bring a baggy t-shirt or night-dress?
- How long will my procedure take?
- How long will I stay at the clinic after my treatment?
- Do I need to bring an overnight bag?
- Will I be in pain during or after my treatment?
- Will I be given painkillers and/or antibiotics to take home?
- Can I drive home?
- Should I be on my own after the treatment?
- How long will the bleeding last after my treatment?
- What painkillers can I take when I get home?
- Should I take a pregnancy test after my treatment and when?
- How long should I wait before having sex again?
- When could I get pregnant again?
- Do I have to come back for a check-up?

Checklist

If you have an abortion, you should take the following to the clinic:

- Any prescribed medication you're taking.
- A blood transfusion card (if you have one).
- Any medical notes or referral letters you have been given.
- Heavy flow sanitary towels (not tampons) for after the procedure.
- Your fee (if you're paying for treatment) – most clinics accept major credit and debit cards, cheques with a guarantee card and cash.
- The numbers of anyone you may wish to contact in case of emergency.

Depending on your treatment, you may also wish to take:

- Change of clothes.
- A small wash bag with soap-free shower gel, shampoo/conditioner, toothbrush, toothpaste, hair brush and a towel so you can freshen up or take a shower after your treatment.
- A book or magazine to read while you're waiting to be seen or for in between treatment.
- If it will make you feel better to apply make-up after the treatment, bring it along.
- A bottle of water and a snack (for after the treatment if you are having an anaesthetic).
- Tissues in case you feel emotional.

Questions for parents, partners and friends

- Can I park at the clinic?
- When will we have to say goodbye before her treatment?
- How long will treatment last?
- Can I wait at the clinic during her treatment?

- Will I be able to talk to someone if I feel emotional or upset?
- Can I buy something to eat, or can I bring my own food?
- Can I use my mobile or laptop in the clinic?
- If I leave while she's receiving treatment, what time should I return?
- Is there anything useful I can bring for when her treatment is complete?
- What can I do to ease any discomfort she feels after the procedure?
- How can I help her recovery in the days ahead?

Checklist

If you're taking your partner, daughter or friend to the clinic, you could take the following:

- Change in case you need to pay for parking.
- A pen and paper to make notes about her aftercare if you need to.
- A book or magazine to read.
- A drink and light snack.
- Tissues in case you feel emotional.
- Flowers or a small gift to give her after the treatment.

Summing Up

- Before you have an abortion it's important to ask questions about anything at all you are unsure of – the staff are there to help and should tell you anything you want or need to know.
- Being well prepared – practically as well as emotionally – will aid your recovery.

The following chapters will now examine the different types of abortion in detail.

Chapter Seven

Medical Abortion

Definition of a medical abortion

A medical abortion involves taking drugs which cause the pregnancy to be expelled from a woman's body in the same way as a natural miscarriage.

Medical abortion may not be suitable if:

- You have an IUD in place (this may need to be removed prior to treatment).
- You have liver, kidney or cardio-vascular disease.
- You take certain anti-inflammatory or blood clotting treatments.
- You suffer from other diseases or illnesses and take other medication.
- You've had a bad or allergic reaction to mifepristone in the past.

'According to Department of Health figures, medical abortions accounted for 35% of the total number of abortions in 2007 compared with 30% in 2006.'

Early medical abortion (EMA)

EMA is done up to the ninth week of pregnancy. It's a nurse-led service in a hospital or clinic and involves taking two drugs, usually at two separate clinic appointments between one and three days apart:

- Mifepristone is taken orally and blocks the action of progesterone, a hormone which sustains pregnancy.
- Misoprostol is a vaginal tablet which contains prostaglandin; prostaglandins occur naturally in the body and can cause your womb to contract.

Preparing for the procedure

As an EMA is similar to a heavy period or natural miscarriage, prepare at home by stocking up on things that make you feel better each month, such as:

- A hot water bottle.
- Painkillers without aspirin (aspirin can increase bleeding).
- Comfy pyjamas.
- Your favourite DVDs, magazines and books.
- Chocolate or other comfort food.

What to take (first visit)

- Your referral letter or medical notes.
- Your fee (if paying).
- Any medication you take routinely.
- Blood transfusion card (if you have one).

Mifepristone

At most clinics mifepristone is taken at the first of a two-stage appointment procedure. After having your checks and going through your notes, a nurse will give you mifepristone to take at the clinic. This will be taken with water.

After you've taken the first tablet, a process has started that cannot be reversed. So if you have any doubts, you must talk to your nurse before you take the mifepristone.

About an hour after taking the tablet, and when the nurse is sure you feel okay, you can go home and continue with normal activities. You can even drive.

- If you experience any pain or discomfort, take paracetamol or ibuprofen (not aspirin as it can increase bleeding).
- If you vomit, make a note of the time and call the clinic for advice.

Side effects

Possible side effects after taking mifepristone are:

- Bleeding and passing of clots.
- Feeling sick or faint.
- Headaches and skin rashes.
- Cramps similar to period pains.

In between treatment

- Occasionally mifepristone causes a miscarriage before the second tablet. You should still go back to the clinic for your second appointment to check everything is okay.
- Once you've taken the first tablet, you're strongly encouraged to take the second.
- Some clinics offer a same day service so you can return to the clinic after six hours for the second tablet or stay there all day. Other clinics ask you to come back one to three days later.
- If you experience any problems or pain in between treatments, ring the clinic, your GP, NHS Direct or visit your local A&E department.

'Although studies so far do not show that mifepristone is associated with any risk of foetal abnormality, women are advised to continue with the abortion once they have taken mifepristone.'
www.fpa.org.uk.

What to take (second visit)

- Any notes you've made about your symptoms since taking the mifepristone.
- Sanitary pads.
- Someone to drive or go home with you.
- Painkillers that do not contain aspirin (which can increase bleeding).

Misoprostol

Before you are given misoprostol, the nurse will ask how you've been since the first treatment and if you've experienced any bleeding or pain. If everything is okay, your treatment can continue:

- Four tablets of misoprostol are inserted into your vagina, usually using a tampon. You'll either do this yourself or a nurse will do it for you.
- Around two to four hours after taking misoprostol, the lining of the womb breaks down and comes out (this may look like small pieces of liver), along with the embryo (sac) and bleeding from the vagina.
- For some women, this feels like strong and sudden period pains with heavy bleeding, others feel little pain and experience light bleeding. It all depends on the individual and stage of pregnancy.
- Your nurse may give you painkillers, or you can take paracetamol or ibuprofen (nothing with aspirin as it can increase bleeding).
- You can usually leave the clinic half an hour after taking the misoprostol – it's best to go home and rest for a couple of hours.

Side effects

Possible side effects after taking misoprostol are:

- Cramps (like period pains) lasting four to six hours after treatment.
- Bleeding similar to a period.
- Heavy bleeding for two to three days. Always use sanitary pads to avoid infection.
- The bleeding should lessen. However, it could last, on and off, for three to four weeks.

My EMA

'When I had an EMA, I was seven weeks pregnant. I had two appointments two days apart and felt normal after taking the mifepristone. I already had a child and I'd experienced an early miscarriage, so the bleeding and stomach cramps about three hours after the misoprostol were manageable. Within an hour or two it was like a normal period. I'd planned to take the next day off work but went in as I felt fine.' Vee, 29.

Risks

There are few risks associated with EMA:

- Excessive bleeding (haemorrhage) happens in around one in every 1,000 abortions.
- Infection is the most common risk.

Contact the clinic or a healthcare professional if you experience:

- Heavy bleeding that soaks through one to two pads in an hour.
- High temperature.
- Vaginal discharge.
- Abdominal pain that doesn't improve after taking painkillers.
- Any other unusual symptoms.

'Women may prefer a medical abortion because the service is nurse-led and they are awake and aware throughout the procedure. They feel more in control.'

Moira Wilson, theatre manager, Calthorpe Clinic.

My daughter's EMA

'My daughter didn't tell me about her abortion. She'd gone to the clinic with her boyfriend. After he dropped her home, she had strong pains and heavy bleeding. She didn't want to tell me, but she was scared and when I offered to call an ambulance she confessed. I was sad she hadn't confided in me but glad I could help. I made a hot water bottle, gave her ibuprofen and lots of cuddles. She was feeling better the next morning, if a little emotional.' Sarah, mum of Kayleigh (17).

Recovery

'Because women are used to periods, they're really well equipped to deal with an EMA. Try not to be frightened if you experience cramping; it means your treatment is working. If you're worried about anything, all registered clinics operate a 24-hour helpline. Although it's beneficial to have support, if a woman needs to conceal her abortion from friends, colleagues or family, it should be easy to do so as an EMA is very similar to a heavy period.' Carolyn Phillips, manager, Calthorpe Clinic.

- Recovery from an EMA is quick but, as with a heavy period, you may feel tired and run-down for a few days.
- Drink lots of water and keep moving as much as you can.
- A hot bath or shower can help you feel better, as can a good night's sleep.
- Always complete your course of antibiotics.
- Do a pregnancy test three weeks after an EMA – any earlier and you may get a false positive result because your hormones are still adjusting. If the result is positive, contact the clinic.
- Rarely, this procedure fails to terminate a pregnancy. If there's any doubt, go back to the clinic for a scan and to discuss another medical procedure or surgical termination.

Getting better

- You can get pregnant as early as one or two weeks after an EMA, so remember to discuss contraception with the clinic.
- Avoid sex for three weeks after the procedure to limit the risk of infection. If you do have sex within this time, use a condom.
- Until your hormones return to normal, and the stress of the situation subsides, you may feel moody or tearful – this is completely normal.
- Although this is a straightforward procedure, don't push yourself too hard. Give yourself a chance to recover, asking for help if you need it.
- Eating a balanced diet, drinking plenty of water and getting some exercise will speed up your recovery.

My partner's EMA

'My girlfriend was angry and kept saying it was my fault. When I tried to go to the clinic, she went ballistic. I sent texts and after a few days she called. She told me she'd bled a lot and that she hadn't wanted me to see her in pain. I respected that.' Neil, partner of Jenny (19).

Medical abortions after nine weeks

A medical abortion may be used after nine weeks, usually if a woman is unable to have anaesthetic. The same drugs used for EMA are administered, but you'll usually be asked to stay in the clinic or hospital rather than going home in between.

As it is later in pregnancy, higher doses of prostaglandin are used and this can cause uncomfortable cramps similar to a late miscarriage. The abortion is usually quick enough for you to return home the same day, but it may be necessary to stay overnight, particularly if you are over 18 weeks.

Very rarely, a medical abortion is performed between 20-24 weeks.

- Most independent clinics perform abortions up to 20 weeks, so this procedure may take place in a hospital or specialist clinic.
- A surgical abortion can still be performed at this stage, but a medical abortion may be used depending on the size of the pregnancy and the suitability of general anaesthetic.
- This procedure takes more time and you will usually stay in the hospital or clinic overnight.
- A doctor will ensure the heart of the foetus is stopped so it is not delivered alive.
- Having a late medical abortion will involve you going through what is similar to labour in order to deliver the foetus. This can be emotionally and physically tiring.

Summing Up

- A medical abortion is a process to end a pregnancy using a combination of drugs.
- Once the drugs have been administered, a medical abortion is similar to miscarriage.
- Medical abortion usually takes place before nine weeks of pregnancy but is occasionally used later if a woman is unable to have a surgical termination.
- Recovery from a medical abortion is usually quick and complications are rare.
- Talk to your GP, clinic or healthcare provider for more information.

Glossary

Contractions: the periodic tightening and relaxing of the womb which can feel like a cramping sensation around the back and/or abdomen.

Embryo: the term used for the foetus before the eighth week of pregnancy.

IUD: a small contraceptive device that is inserted into the womb, also known as 'the coil'.

Miscarriage: when a pregnancy ends naturally before a foetus can survive outside the womb.

Chapter Eight

Vacuum Aspiration Abortion

Definition of a vacuum aspiration abortion

Commonly used between seven and 15 weeks of pregnancy, vacuum aspiration (or suction termination) uses gentle suction to remove the products of pregnancy from the womb.

There are two types of suction termination:

- Manual – this procedure uses a syringe to apply suction and is suitable up to 10 weeks. Manual suction is usually used if a woman wants a surgical procedure before eight weeks.
- Machine – a hollow tube (cannula) is passed into the womb and attached to a bottle and mechanical pump, providing a gentle vacuum to remove pregnancy tissue.

'A manual vacuum has two main advantages: the surgeon can see the products of the pregnancy and check everything has been removed, and the procedure is not noisy, unlike machine suction, which is helpful if a woman chooses local anaesthetic.' Moira Wilson, theatre manager, Calthorpe Clinic.

Length of procedure

The procedure usually takes between five to 10 minutes. It can be carried out under local or general anaesthetic, depending on the stage of pregnancy and the woman's personal choice.

A vacuum aspiration is usually carried out as day-care in a hospital or independent clinic. Discharge times differ depending on the stage of pregnancy.

Vacuum aspiration abortion may not be suitable if:

- You are unable to have an anaesthetic.
- Your pregnancy is too large for this method.
- You have a Body Mass Index (BMI) over 40.

Your doctor will discuss your medical history with you to make sure a surgical procedure is appropriate.

Vacuum aspiration with local anaesthetic

- Local anaesthetic is available under 12 weeks of pregnancy.
- The anaesthetic is given around the womb's entrance.
- Recovery is quick and after resting you may be able to leave the clinic within an hour or two.
- Many clinics will offer you the choice of a general or local anaesthetic – although a local anaesthetic is considered safer, having it applied can be uncomfortable and many women prefer to be 'asleep'. If you change your mind at the last minute, the consultant anaesthetist should discuss a general anaesthetic with you.

Vacuum aspiration with general anaesthetic

- A general anaesthetic means you will be 'asleep' during the procedure.
- A general anaesthetic can always be used with this procedure.

Vacuum aspiration with conscious sedation

- Some clinics now offer women the choice of conscious sedation.

- Conscious sedation makes you sleepy, but you'll be conscious during the procedure.

'When women choose local anaesthetic, we advise them to take a mixture of pain relief and antibiotics before the procedure. This is administered as a rectal suppository which some women don't like the idea of. It's very effective, however, lasting much longer than intravenous pain relief.' Moira Wilson, theatre manager, Calthorpe Clinic.

Preparing for the procedure

- You will be advised not to eat anything for a period of time before the treatment.
- You should still be able to drink water up until two hours before your appointment time.
- Avoid smoking for as long as possible before treatment.
- You will usually be asked to remove jewellery and piercings before treatment, but items that cannot be removed can be taped over.

'I could have had a general anaesthetic but I wanted to be awake and to see what was happening to me during the procedure.'

Shamim, 22.

What to take

- Your referral letter or medical notes.
- Your fee (if paying).
- Any medication you take routinely.
- Blood transfusion card (if you have one).
- Although this is likely to be day-care treatment, you could pack a small bag with a change of clothes and toiletries and take a shower afterwards.
- You may wear a hospital gown, but ask if you can bring a night-dress or loose-fitting t-shirt.

The procedure

If you're having a manual suction procedure:

- If you're having a general anaesthetic, this is given before the manual suction procedure begins and you'll be taken to a recovery room afterwards where you will regain consciousness quickly.
- If you're having a local anaesthetic, you'll be asked to position yourself on an exam table in the same position used for a pelvic exam (lying on your back with your feet in stirrups).
- A local anaesthetic will be injected into the cervix – this can feel uncomfortable.
- Sometimes a small instrument is used to dilate (open) the cervix slightly – but this is rare under 12 weeks.
- A thin tube is passed into your womb. A handheld syringe is attached to suction the pregnancy tissue out.

Possible side effects during a manual suction procedure:

- Most women feel cramping during the procedure. The cramps will lessen after the tube is removed.
- Some women also experience nausea, sweating or feeling faint.

If you're having a mechanical vacuum aspiration procedure:

- Misoprostol tablets may be placed into your vagina before the procedure to soften the cervix – this usually happens from 12 weeks of pregnancy. This can cause some discomfort (usually cramps and nausea) before the operation begins.
- If you're having a general anaesthetic, this is given before the vacuum aspiration procedure begins and you'll be taken to a recovery room afterwards where you will regain consciousness quickly.
- If you're having a local anaesthetic (under 12 weeks), you'll be asked to position yourself on the exam table in the same position used for a pelvic exam (lying on your back with your feet in stirrups).

- A local anaesthetic is injected into the cervix – this can feel uncomfortable. Additional medicine for pain may be given orally or intravenously. Medicines that slow bleeding may also be mixed with the local anaesthetic.
- A thin, hollow tube (cannula) is passed into the cervix and a gentle vacuum attached to a small machine or pump will draw the pregnancy tissue out of the womb. The machine can be noisy.

Possible side effects during a mechanical suction procedure:

- Most women feel cramping during the procedure. The cramps should lessen after the tube is removed.
- Some women may also experience nausea, sweating or feeling faint.

After treatment

- After your procedure you'll be taken to a recovery room where you can rest until the anaesthetic wears off (10-20 minutes). Some clinics use an extended recovery room where you can relax until you can get dressed. You should have the opportunity to shower or freshen up which will help your short-term recovery.
- You may feel hungry and should be offered something light to eat (often toast) and a drink.
- You'll be assessed by a nurse or doctor before being discharged. Discharge times depend on the type of anaesthetic used, stage of pregnancy and clinic policy.
- Before you leave you should be given information and advice on aftercare and antibiotics. This is a good time to ask any questions about recovery.
- You cannot drive for 24 hours after the procedure, so it's advisable to get a taxi or arrange for someone to take you home.

'We use a very light general anaesthetic which can be administered within 30 seconds through the back of the hand. Women are awake and recovering within 10 minutes of their treatment.'

Moira Wilson, theatre manager, Calthorpe Clinic.

My vacuum aspiration procedure

'I had a planned pregnancy but found out at the 12-week scan that the foetus had died. The doctor explained it was a missed miscarriage because my body hadn't expelled the pregnancy naturally. I had a vacuum aspiration procedure the following week under a general anaesthetic. Although I didn't choose to have an abortion, the procedure was quick and I only felt uncomfortable for a couple of hours afterwards, which made it easier to cope with.' Jan, 35.

Risks

Vacuum aspiration abortion is a safe procedure. However, no medical or surgical procedure is entirely risk free.

- Problems at the time of abortion are rare, but the later in the pregnancy you have the procedure, the more likely you are to have complications.
- Excessive bleeding (haemorrhage) happens in around one in every 1,000 abortions.
- Damage to the cervix happens in no more than 10 in every 1,000 abortions.
- Damage to the womb at the time of surgical abortions happens in up to four in every 1,000 abortions.

Contact the clinic or a healthcare professional if you experience:

- Heavy bleeding that soaks through one to two pads in an hour.
- High temperature.
- Vaginal discharge.
- Abdominal pain that doesn't improve after taking painkillers.
- Any other unusual symptoms.

My daughter's vacuum aspiration

'I used to work on the gynaecological ward of a local hospital, so when my daughter had a termination, I offered to go with her. I think I gave good advice on what to expect and suggested questions we could ask, but I was surprised that the procedure is much quicker than it used to be. Even though she had a general, she was back on her feet within an hour of the operation.' Glenda, mum of Ashanti (27).

Recovery

- After the procedure you may bleed heavily, experience stomach cramps and pass clots for two to three days. If the bleeding is excessive or doesn't slow down, contact your GP or clinic.
- If you feel uncomfortable, you can take any painkiller, such as paracetamol or ibuprofen, which does not contain aspirin (as this can increase bleeding). Do not take more than two in four hours.
- It's very important that you take the antibiotics the clinic or hospital supply you with as instructed. They help to reduce the risk of infection.
- Recovery is quick but, as with a heavy period, you may feel tired, run-down and low for a few days. The anaesthetic may also make you feel tired and even weepy for a few hours or days after the procedure.
- It's rare that surgical abortion fails to remove a pregnancy, but it's always wise to do a pregnancy test around three weeks after the abortion for your own peace of mind.
- If any pregnancy tissue is retained (which can cause prolonged bleeding or discomfort), you may be required to have a dilation and curettage (D&C) procedure during which a surgeon will clear any remaining tissue from the womb using a sharp surgical instrument. This procedure is performed under a general anaesthetic.

'Overall, just over two out of every 1,000 women who have a surgical abortion continue to be pregnant.'

Royal College of Obstetricians and Gynaecologists (RCOG), 2004.

Getting better

- You can get pregnant again one to two weeks after a vacuum aspiration procedure, so contraception is crucial. You may be able to have Depo-Provera, IUCD, IUS or Implanon at the same time as surgery (see glossary). This may be available on the NHS, even if you have your treatment in a private clinic.

- Avoid sex for three weeks after the procedure to limit the risk of infection. If you do have sex within this time, use a condom.
- You may feel emotional for a few days (or longer depending on the stage of pregnancy) as your hormones settle down. The stress of the situation can also heighten emotions. This is completely normal.
- Don't push yourself in the days and weeks afterwards if you feel vulnerable. Give yourself chance to recover and ask for help and support.
- Eating a balanced diet, drinking plenty of water and getting some exercise when you feel well enough will speed up your recovery.

My partner's vacuum aspiration abortion

'I was terrified when Izzy had an abortion at 14 weeks. We hadn't told her parents, so as well as worrying that something would go wrong for Izzy's sake, I was also scared that I'd have to call them to the clinic and they'd hate me more than they already did. While Izzy was in theatre, I talked to one of the nurses and she reassured me about how safe it was and how quickly Izzy would be feeling better.' James, ex-partner of Izzy (22).

Summing Up

- A vacuum aspiration abortion is a surgical process to end a pregnancy.
- The pregnancy is removed from the womb using a gentle suction method, either manually with a syringe (up to 10 weeks) or mechanically with a pump.
- Recovery from a vacuum aspiration abortion is usually quick and complications are rare.

Glossary

Body Mass Index: a mathematical formula that takes into account a person's height and weight.

Depo-Provera: a contraceptive injection given every three months.

Implanon: a matchstick-sized plastic device that is put under the skin of your arm and prevents pregnancy for up to three years.

Intravenous: putting liquid substances directly into a vein.

IUCD: an intrauterine (in the womb) contraceptive device.

IUS: a small t-shaped plastic device which is placed in the womb. It slowly releases a progestogen hormone to prevent pregnancy.

Local anaesthetic: medicine used to numb a small part of the body.

Chapter Nine

Dilation and Evacuation and Late Abortions

Definition of surgical dilation and evacuation (D&E)

From around 15 weeks of pregnancy, the cervix is gently dilated (stretched and opened) so the pregnancy can be removed in fragments using a suction tube and special forceps. The procedure is performed using a general anaesthetic and once the cervix is open the process is the same as the vacuum aspiration method.

Length of procedure

Around three hours before the operation you'll be given drugs to soften the cervix. The procedure itself takes 10-20 minutes and, if you're healthy and there are no complications, you should be back on your feet within an hour or two.

A D&E is usually carried out as day-care in a hospital or independent clinic. Discharge times differ depending on the stage of pregnancy and clinic policy.

D&E abortion may not be suitable if:

- You are unable to have an anaesthetic.
- Your pregnancy is too large for this method.
- You have a Body Mass Index (BMI) over 40.

Your doctor will discuss your medical history with you to make sure a surgical procedure is appropriate.

General anaesthetic

- A general anaesthetic means you will be 'asleep' during the procedure.
- You're usually given the anaesthetic via a needle in the back of your hand.

'The vast majority of abortion surgeons available are men. These surgeons are highly trained experts but, unfortunately, if a woman feels uncomfortable about a man performing the procedure, she is unlikely to be able to request a female surgeon. She will be supported by nurses throughout treatment, who are very likely to be female, and a request to have a female nurse present should be possible to meet. Female staff members are usually in theatre to assist the surgeon.' Moira Wilson, theatre manager, Calthorpe Clinic.

'Of the 198,499 abortions performed in 2007, just 2,927 were carried out after 20 weeks.'

Department of Health.

Preparing for the procedure

- You're usually advised not to eat anything from midnight on the night before your treatment.
- You should still be able to drink water up until two hours before your appointment time.
- Avoid smoking for as long as possible before treatment.
- You're usually asked to remove jewellery and piercings, but items that cannot be removed will be taped over.

What to take

- Your referral letter or medical notes.
- Your fee (if paying).
- Any medication you take routinely.
- Blood transfusion card (if you have one).

- Although this is likely to be day-care treatment, you could pack a small bag with a change of clothes and toiletries so you can take a shower afterwards.
- You may wear a hospital gown, but ask if you can bring a night-dress or loose-fitting t-shirt.

The procedure

- At the clinic you may be asked to take misoprostol, the drug used during early medical abortion (EMA), to soften and prepare your cervix for dilation. This is usually placed inside the vagina using a tampon.
- If you are over 18 weeks, you may also be given dilapan, a thin rod which can be used to dilate and ripen the cervix. This process, like the misoprostol, can cause the womb to contract and feel uncomfortable. Some women experience nausea, but it will make the surgery easier and safer.
- You should be able to walk to theatre where you will be prepared for your general anaesthetic.
- Once your anaesthetic has taken effect, your cervix will be gently stretched and the pregnancy will be broken-up using special instruments.
- Suction will then be used to remove the pregnancy in the same way as a vacuum aspiration abortion.
- Although D&E can be used until 24 weeks, most clinics are licensed to perform abortions to 20 weeks, so the procedure may take place at a specialist clinic or hospital after this time.

After treatment

- After your procedure you should be taken to a recovery room where you can rest until the anaesthetic wears off (10-20 minutes). Some clinics use an extended recovery room where you can relax until you can get dressed. You should have the opportunity to shower or freshen up which will help your short-term recovery.
- You may feel hungry and should be offered something light to eat (often toast) and a drink.

- You'll be assessed by a nurse or doctor before being discharged. Discharge times depend on the stage of the pregnancy, your individual recovery and clinic policy.
- Before you leave you should be given information and advice on aftercare and antibiotics. This is a good time to ask any questions about recovery.
- You cannot drive for 24 hours, so it's advisable to get a taxi or arrange for someone to take you home.

'Finding out I was 18 weeks pregnant worried me because I imagined a baby inside me, not just a blob. I pushed it out of my mind because I desperately didn't want to be a teenage mum.'

Naz, 17.

My D&E procedure

'I thought I was eight weeks pregnant but an ultrasound showed I was 19 weeks and six days. I was shocked but still wanted a termination. The most difficult part of the day was after misoprostol tablets and dilapan were inserted using a tampon. I felt sick and in pain and couldn't wait to get to the operating table. Luckily, I met a girl who was a couple of years younger than me. She was 18 weeks pregnant. We went through the procedure together, waking up around the same time in the recovery room. Having someone to talk to helped me get through the day.' Gillian, 21.

'Lots of women bond with other clients on the day. We hear women chatting and comparing experiences. It's not a fun day out, but knowing you're not the only one helps a great deal.' Carolyn Phillips, manager, Calthorpe Clinic.

Risks

D&E abortion is a safe procedure but no medical or surgical procedure is entirely risk free.

- Problems at the time of abortion are rare, but the later in the pregnancy you have the procedure, the more likely you are to have complications.
- Excessive bleeding (haemorrhage) happens in around one in every 1,000 abortions.
- Damage to the cervix happens in no more than 10 in every 1,000 abortions.
- Damage to the womb at the time of surgical abortions happens in up to four in every 1,000 abortions.

My daughter's D&E abortion

'When my daughter told me she was pregnant, we sat down with her boyfriend and his parents to talk through her options. We all agreed abortion would be for the best, but in the end it was a long and emotional day. I was worried about her and couldn't help feeling sad and guilty because this could have been my grandchild. Going through the experience has brought us closer, and I respected her boyfriend for sticking by her. She is already a more mature woman as a result.' Linda, mum of Evie (16).

Recovery

- After the procedure you may bleed heavily, experience stomach cramps and pass clots for two to three days. If the bleeding doesn't slow down or hasn't stopped after two to three weeks, contact your GP or clinic.
- If you feel uncomfortable you can take any painkiller, such as paracetamol or ibuprofen, which does not contain aspirin (as this can increase bleeding). Do not take more than two in four hours.
- It's very important that you take the antibiotics the clinic or hospital supply you with as instructed. They help to reduce the risk of infection.
- Recovery can be fast but, as with a heavy period, you may feel tired, run-down and low for a few days. The anaesthetic may also make you feel tired and even weepy for a few hours or days after the procedure.
- If any pregnancy tissue is retained (which can cause prolonged bleeding or discomfort), you may be required to have a dilation and curettage (D&C) procedure during which a surgeon will clear any remaining tissue from the womb using a sharp surgical instrument. This procedure is performed under a general anaesthetic.

Getting better

- You can get pregnant again from one to two weeks after a D&E, so contraception is crucial. You can have Depo-Provera, IUCD, IUS or Implanon at the same time as surgery (see glossary). This may be available on the NHS, even if you have your treatment in a private clinic.
- Avoid sex for at least three weeks after the procedure to limit the risk of infection. If you do have sex within this time, use a condom.
- You may feel emotional for a few days or weeks as your hormones settle down to their pre-pregnancy levels. The stress of the situation can also heighten emotions. This is all completely normal.

'Instead of criticising a woman's decision to have a late termination, with no knowledge of the details, we could say that to undergo the procedure she will have given it much thought and must have had very pressing reasons.'

Penny Barber, chief executive, Brook in Birmingham.

My partner's D&E abortion

'My partner had a D&E at 16 weeks. I offered to support her if she went ahead with the pregnancy but was relieved when she decided not to. Going through the experience made us stronger as a couple. When we planned pregnancy together later and experienced a miscarriage, we did wonder if the abortion was in some way to blame. We eventually had a healthy son and feel we became parents at exactly the right time.' Ed, partner of Michaela (34).

Abortion 20 to 24 weeks

Abortion at this stage is not common. There are two options and both involve foeticide. This means a doctor stops the foetus' heart before the procedure so it is not delivered alive.

Surgical two-stage abortion

- The two stages of this procedure each require a general anaesthetic.
- During the first stage, the heart of the foetus will be stopped and the cervix softened.
- The following day the foetus and surrounding tissue will be removed using the D&E method.

- Surgical two-stage abortions usually require an overnight stay in hospital.

Medically induced abortion

- A medically induced abortion at this stage is similar to a late natural miscarriage and usually involves an overnight stay in hospital.
- Prostaglandin is injected into the womb, causing it to contract strongly (like in labour) until the foetus is delivered. This can last between six and 12 hours. You'll remain awake and can take medication to control the pain.
- Afterwards, a D&E or dilation and curettage (D&C) procedure may be used to ensure the womb is completely empty.
- This process can be physically and emotionally draining and most women need time to recover. They may require some additional counselling if they feel distressed afterwards.

Dealing with late abortion

Later abortions are longer and often more complex. Women with irregular periods, very young women, women using new contraception and women finding it difficult to deal with sexual exploitation, abuse or rape may not find out that they are pregnant until a later stage. They have less time to decide and are usually very shocked and confused.

Abortions between 20 to 24 weeks may also be performed due to foetal abnormalities picked up at the 20 week scan in a planned pregnancy. In these cases, women may need additional support to cope with the process and recover physically and emotionally from their bereavement. For specialist help contact:

- Antenatal Results and Choices (www.arc-uk.org).
- Sands (www.uk-sands.org).
- Cruse Bereavement Care (www.crusebereavementcare.org.uk).
- Child Bereavement Charity (www.childbereavement.org.uk).

'According to Department of Health figures for 2007, 1,900 abortions (1% of the annual total) were performed on the grounds that there was a risk the child would be born handicapped.'

My late abortion

'I was in my 40s when I became pregnant unexpectedly for the fourth time. My three children were teenagers, but we all came to terms with the pregnancy. At the 20 week scan, my doctor detected a serious and inoperable heart defect. The baby was very unlikely to survive. I reluctantly requested an abortion and was admitted to hospital at 22 weeks for a medical termination. I'd been through labour but it was a punishing process without the reward of a healthy baby. I never felt guilty because I believe I saved my baby, who I named and held a memorial service for, a great deal of pain and suffering.' Charlie, 47.

'Anti-abortion groups lobby to reduce the time limit for abortions, but that would also reduce the time a woman has to make her decision; a decision that is not black and white and can take a long time.'

Ann Furedi, chief executive, BPAS.

Summing Up

- A dilation and evacuation abortion is a surgical process ending a pregnancy.
- The pregnancy is broken up in the womb and removed using gentle suction and special forceps.
- An abortion between 20 and 24 weeks is rare but can take place in a hospital or specialist clinic, using a medical or surgical method.

Glossary

Bereavement: a state of sorrow or mourning over the death or loss of a loved one.

Body Mass Index: a mathematical formula that takes into account a person's height and weight.

Depo-Provera: a contraceptive injection given every three months.

Forceps: a handheld, hinged instrument used for grasping and holding objects.

Implanon: a matchstick-sized plastic device that is put under the skin of your arm and prevents pregnancy for up to three years.

IUCD: an intrauterine (in the womb) contraceptive device.

IUS: a small t-shaped plastic device which is placed in the womb. It slowly releases a progestogen hormone to prevent pregnancy.

Labour: the final stage of pregnancy, leading to childbirth.

Chapter Ten

Supporting Someone Through Abortion

If you're supporting a woman during an abortion

- Although an abortion is a relatively short and simple procedure, she has experienced a pregnancy loss and deserves care, kindness and support.
- If you have questions to ask at the clinic, discuss them with her first; although you may be curious, her own questions are most important.
- If you're nervous about going to the clinic, consider ringing ahead for a chat or even visiting beforehand so you know what to expect.
- Follow staff guidance in the clinic and respect their policy. It's unlikely that you'll be able to stay with her during treatment and every clinic or hospital will want at least a short time alone with a woman to ensure the decision to have a termination is her own. Being difficult or pushy will not make the experience any easier for her.
- Although flowers or chocolates may be appreciated, love and support is more important than material gifts.

If you're supporting a woman after an abortion

- Offer flexible support; she may feel great and want to move on quickly, or want to be pampered and take it easy. Ask her what she wants and try to offer her options.
- Don't be surprised if she recovers quickly – but prepare to be patient; if she had surgery, she may need time to bounce back.
- Make sure she knows she can contact you at any time, but respect her wishes; she may need space to come to terms with what's happened.
- Although you may want to take action to help her recover, she may just want her emotions to be acknowledged – or she may simply need a hug.
- If her behaviour is erratic, try not to take what she says to heart. She's been through an exhausting decision-making process and an unplanned pregnancy is a stressful experience.
- Wait until she's feeling better before having heavy discussions about the future.
- Don't force her to undertake counselling if she doesn't want to, or isn't ready.
- If she feels bereaved, remember that whatever reasons were behind her termination, she has suffered a pregnancy loss. If she wants to bury the foetus or commemorate it in some way (see chapter 12), try to support her decision. She's finding coping strategies for her grief and this is healthy.
- If you're a partner and you feel guilty, or the termination has affected you deeply, try to be honest (yet tactful) about your feelings. It may give her comfort to know she's not experiencing this alone.
- If you need someone to talk to, consider contacting one of the organisations listed in this book.

Summing Up

- Your physical presence and moral support can make her abortion much easier to deal with and recover from.
- Supporting someone through an abortion can be emotionally draining – if you need some help and support, don't be afraid to ask for it.

Chapter Eleven

Your Health After Abortion

Recovering from abortion

'Although I experienced stronger cramps than I expected after my abortion at 14 weeks, I bounced back quickly. I had a general anaesthetic and felt a bit rough for a day or so, but my bleeding slowed within hours. I had a bloody discharge for a couple of weeks, so I went to my GP. She sent me for a scan but everything was fine. I had my period as normal five weeks after the operation. The relief that everything was over helped me heal physically.' Maggie, 26.

There's no such thing as a completely 'risk free' clinical procedure, but abortion is statistically very safe and poses few risks to a woman's physical health, particularly when carried out during the first 12 weeks of pregnancy.

For the vast majority of women, recovery is quick and uncomplicated.

If you develop any unexpected symptoms or reactions, contact your clinic or GP immediately.

- After an abortion you will usually continue to experience bleeding for at least a few days.
- The bleeding can vary from light to heavy, depending on the type of procedure you've had and stage of pregnancy.
- The bleeding shouldn't be any worse than your heaviest period and is

usually accompanied by period-type pains. If you need some pain relief you can take paracetamol or ibuprofen (or any painkiller without aspirin, as this can encourage bleeding). Do not take more than two in four hours.

- It's normal to pass small clots for a few days after the operation.
- A small amount of bleeding may continue for three to four weeks – don't use tampons until your next period, use sanitary pads instead. This reduces the risk of infection.
- If you experience very heavy bleeding (soaking one to two pads in an hour), contact your GP or clinic immediately.

'Two days after my abortion, I started to bleed heavily. I had pelvic pain and a very high fever. My mum called an emergency doctor and he told me I'd contracted a pelvic infection.'

Rosa, 38.

Risks after abortion

- Infection is the most common problem after abortion.
- If bleeding or pain is severe, you have a raised temperature or unusual vaginal discharge, this could mean you have an infection – call the clinic or your GP as soon as possible.
- The most likely cause of infection is an existing STI such as chlamydia or gonorrhea.
- If a woman has an abortion when she has an STI it can lead to pelvic infection. This can cause infertility, increased risk of ectopic pregnancy and chronic pelvic inflammatory disease (PID).
- Many STIs (including chlamydia, the most common STI) can be present without symptoms, and even if you've only had unprotected sex once, you can still pick them up.
- It is very important to be tested (at least for chlamydia) before an abortion.

Aftercare advice

The hospital or clinic will give you advice about aftercare as well as antibiotics. It's important to follow this advice so you can recover completely and quickly:

- Advice will be given on how to reduce the risk of infection. This will include avoiding having sex for three weeks after your treatment.

- Although you may feel fine, it's best to take things easy at first, avoiding strenuous activity (such as heavy lifting or aerobic exercise) for about two weeks.
- You can have a warm bath or shower whenever you want, but avoid using bath oils and bubble bath at first and don't soak in a hot bath until the bleeding has stopped.
- Avoid public swimming pools for at least two weeks to limit the risk of infection.
- You won't necessarily have a follow-up appointment but if you have any concerns you can request a check-up, either with your GP or a local clinic.
- Do a pregnancy test after three weeks (allowing your hormones to go back to their normal levels) for your own peace of mind.

Your fertility after an abortion

- Your first period usually arrives four to six weeks after an abortion, depending on the type of contraception you're using. It may be heavier than usual.
- You could get pregnant as early as one or two weeks after an abortion, so use reliable contraception as soon as you start to have sex again.
- You can start taking the pill or mini-pill immediately. Antibiotics can affect how oestrogen (the pill's active ingredient) is absorbed into your body, so use condoms or another additional method of contraception until you've finished your course of antibiotics.
- If you were taking the pill and it failed, discuss alternative methods or taking it again with your GP or family planning clinic.
- You may be able to have a long-acting contraceptive at the same time as your abortion. The NHS may pay for this, even if you're having private treatment. Your clinic or local family planning service should give you further information.

'Before my termination I stacked up on DVDs and healthy food so I didn't have to leave the house for a couple of days. I just needed that time to catch my breath and take it easy.'

Sital, 27.

Long-term risks to your fertility

- The earlier in pregnancy an abortion is performed, the less likely there are to be complications.
- If you have an abortion with no complications, there should be no reason to worry about your chances of becoming pregnant or having a baby in the future.
- According to www.nhs.co.uk, research into medical abortion shows that it doesn't affect your fertility and there is no increased risk of future miscarriage.
- In rare cases of surgical abortion, the suction process can cause scarring of the womb. This can be treated with a relatively simple operation to repair the scarring.
- Very rarely, a surgical abortion can weaken the cervix. If your cervix is weakened, you may have an increased risk of future miscarriage due to 'cervical incompetence', a rare condition where your cervix can't stay tightly closed during pregnancy. If this happens, you may need an operation in which a small stitch is made in the neck of your cervix to help keep it closed.

Rebalancing hormones

Every woman's body is different, so while some may feel back to normal very quickly, others have to wait longer before their hormones return to pre-pregnancy levels.

- The hormones your body produced to sustain a pregnancy may have triggered morning sickness, mood swings, sore breasts, fatigue and changes to your normal appetite and sleep patterns. For some women, these symptoms stop immediately, for others it takes a few days or weeks.
- It's likely you'll still test positive on a pregnancy test for up to three weeks after a termination.
- Depending on the stage of your pregnancy, you may still 'feel' pregnant and swollen for a few days – this is normal. However, if you have any concerns, make sure you contact your GP or clinic.

- Your first period after an abortion may be an emotional time, but the feeling will pass.

Seeing a GP after an abortion

'After a termination, some women feel emotionally and physically affected by the experience, however smooth the process was. As a general practitioner, I am able to support them on any level required. Occasionally, if a medical problem or complication arises, such as an infection, we will investigate and treat it accordingly. If we feel more specialist advice is needed we can refer on appropriately. At the same time as addressing any physical or emotional issues, we try to offer all round care and support for the future, discussing contraceptive options available and also sexual health advice.' Dr Charlotte Zoltonos, GP.

- Even if your GP would not refer you for an abortion on moral grounds, there is no reason why he or she should refuse to treat you if any complications arise after your treatment.
- If you wish to make a complaint about your GP, contact the Healthcare Commission (www.healthcarecommission.org.uk).

Getting better checklist

As your body settles down, be kind to yourself and don't expect an immediate recovery. Get as much rest as you can and take the following steps to help your body return to normal:

- Eat a balanced diet, increasing your intake of protein (e.g. meat, poultry, fish, cheese, tofu and nuts) which helps your body to heal and stabilises your blood sugar.
- If you've lost your appetite, snack on protein rich foods, fresh vegetables and fruit to bolster your immune system.
- If you've been given a follow-up appointment, it's important to keep it so you can discuss how you're feeling emotionally and physically.

Getting back to normal

- After an abortion, going back to school or work may feel like a big step.
- If you've taken time off without giving the real reason for your absence, you may feel uncomfortable with friends and colleagues at first, but you have every right to your privacy and, in time, you'll relate to them normally again.
- You shouldn't rush back to school or work if you don't feel physically able. However, resuming your usual routine will help you recover.

If you have a busy life and feel overwhelmed, try these tips for getting back into the swing:

- Break down your day into small tasks to make it more manageable.
- Delegate jobs or ask for extra help when you need it.
- If you have a good friend or colleague you can confide in, it may help to share your experience so you have someone to sound-off with as you settle back in.
- If there's a counsellor at work or school, take advantage; book an appointment and talk through your feelings. Even one session can help and you should be offered complete confidentiality.

'32% of women undergoing abortions in 2007 had one or more previous abortions. The proportion has risen from about 28% since 1997.'

Department of Health.

Multiple abortions

'I've had three terminations over the course of five years. The first two pregnancies happened after a condom split and in spite of me taking the morning after pill. The third was utterly surprising; we'd used a condom and, as far as I was aware, nothing had gone wrong. After my second abortion I completely changed my behaviour, being very careful about getting sexually involved with men. It seemed all the more unfair that it happened again and led to feelings of guilt; going through two abortions is awful, but three looks like a habit. The sense of shame was overwhelming. I wondered how I could ever tell a man I loved, and expect him to love me back. It upset me so much that I had two months of weekly therapy sessions. I feel a lot lighter having spoken to a professional and can now say that I'm not to blame; I have just been very unlucky.' Roni, 31.

- There is no evidence that having more than one abortion can affect your fertility, although (according to www.nhs.co.uk) you may have a slightly increased risk of future miscarriage.
- After an abortion it makes sense to review your chosen method of contraception, but accidents can happen more than once, so try not to be too hard on yourself if you're unfortunate enough to experience another unwanted pregnancy.
- If you feel stressed, low or stigmatised because you have had more than one abortion, consider seeking professional counselling to deal with your feelings and cope with the reactions of others.

'Instead of condemning the one in three women having a termination who have had one before, we must identify and overcome the barriers that prevent these women accessing reliable contraception.'

Penny Barber, chief executive, Brook in Birmingham.

Summing Up

- Abortion is statistically safe and poses few short and long-term health risks.
- You'll be given lots of advice on aftercare by your healthcare provider and can boost your recovery by eating well, exercising and talking through your feelings.
- There is no evidence to suggest that abortion will affect your ability to get pregnant again or have a baby in the future.

Glossary

Clots: blood clotting is a natural process in which blood cells rapidly form a clump to regulate a flow of blood.

Contraception: any method used to stop a woman getting pregnant, including condoms, the pill and the coil.

Immune system: the cells, proteins, tissues and organs that defend people against germs and infections.

Infertility: being unable to conceive a child.

Pelvic inflammatory disease: a generic term for inflammation of the female uterus, fallopian tubes and/or ovaries.

Sexually transmitted infection (STI): an illness passed to another through sexual contact.

Chapter Twelve

Moving On

No regrets

'My abortion was the right thing to do. I'd split-up with the father of my first child but he refused to move out; the inevitable happened. My daughter was little and I didn't want another child to look after by myself or to stretch my already limited income. While I did feel sad, particularly as it wasn't that long since I'd had an exciting pregnancy, I never had regrets. My ex proved he wasn't fit to have another child immediately when he had to be persuaded to pick me up from the clinic and refused to pay for a cab home. When I married again and got pregnant, I did occasionally worry that something would go wrong as 'punishment' for the abortion, but the rational side of me quickly dismissed that. Having a planned pregnancy under such different circumstances, with a fabulous partner, confirmed that I made the right decision.' Geena, 33.

Mixed emotions

After an abortion you'll probably feel a mixture of emotions. The more informed you are about the procedure before you have it, the less severe your emotional reaction tends to be.

You may feel incredibly relieved the pregnancy is over but, even if you were confident about your decision, it's not unusual to feel a sense of sadness when a pregnancy ends. If it was a difficult decision, or you had an abortion because there was a problem with your health or the foetus, you may experience powerful feelings of loss and regret. It's important to talk about these feelings and seek professional support if they affect your health or show no sign of lessening in time.

Some women feel emotionally numb after an abortion; this is another common reaction. It's better to let your emotions out rather than bottling them up, but you should never force an emotional reaction; for some women, an abortion is an event they can move on from quickly, without problems.

Any emotional response is best handled if you have a good network of support around you. It's not healthy to suppress your feelings, so even if you're determined to put on a brave face, be kind to yourself, asking for help if you need it.

'I knew I was making the right decision, but it still took some time to adjust afterwards. I only had to wait a week for my abortion, but in that time I'd got used to feeling pregnant and I did miss it when it was over.'

Emily, 25.

Difficult times

For many women, certain times in life may be emotionally difficult after an abortion, regardless of why they had the termination.

- Your first period after an abortion is a reminder that you're not pregnant anymore and may be particularly difficult if the pregnancy was planned.
- Many women feel emotional around the time the baby would have been due. This may build-up as the date approaches, so try to pre-empt your response by getting good support in place.
- Your emotions may be triggered by the anniversary of the abortion – again, if you anticipate this being an emotional time, plan to be with good friends or family who can offer support.
- When women go on to have planned pregnancies and reach the stage at which they had a previous abortion, some report feeling sad, anxious or guilty. It helps to look back at your circumstances when you had the abortion and the reasons behind your decision. It may also be helpful to read any diaries or letters you kept at the time. It's likely that your situation is different now and it's important to remember that.
- When women go on to plan a pregnancy, they may worry that they either won't be able to conceive or will miscarry as a 'punishment' for an abortion. Studies show that abortion is a very safe procedure and the vast majority

of women go on to have normal, healthy pregnancies when they want to. If you're worried, mention it to your GP or midwife. They should be able to put your mind at rest.

Bereavement

Like a miscarriage or stillbirth, abortion can be experienced as a bereavement, particularly (but by no means exclusively) if the pregnancy was planned.

Even if you didn't want to be pregnant, an abortion is the end of something. It may help to look at it as a new beginning, but if you need time to mourn your loss, don't feel afraid or embarrassed to ask friends, family or colleagues for it.

- Whatever your reasons, the fact that you decided to end your pregnancy doesn't mean you're not allowed to grieve.
- If your pregnancy was planned and you had to make difficult decisions about abortion for medical reasons, this can add another dimension to the emotions of your bereavement. The charity Antenatal Results and Choices (www.arc-uk.org) can help you deal with the aftermath of a loss after a diagnosis of foetal abnormality.
- Joining a support group, chatting to friends or contributing to an online forum can help you come to terms with your loss.
- Anyone who feels they need help coping with bereavement can contact Cruse Bereavement Care (www.crusebereavementcare.org.uk).

Saying goodbye

For some women, whatever their reasons for having an abortion, it is important to mark the end of their pregnancy and to commemorate the foetus in some way.

- If you want to take away the remains of the foetus to bury, the hospital or clinic should facilitate this for you and will provide a sealed, opaque container.
- Many women who travel from other countries to have an abortion wish to take the remains of their pregnancy home with them. You should be able to

put the container in your hold luggage and the clinic should give you a letter explaining what the container is so you don't have to face any awkward questions from customs.

- Some women find it helpful to plant a tree or flower. This can be helpful if you want to be reminded of the pregnancy.
- Other women write a letter or poem, explaining their reasons for ending the pregnancy. Even if they then throw the letter away or never read it again, some women find this therapeutic.

Good mental health

- Immediately after your abortion, you might feel emotional or down. Hormonal changes and the stress of an unplanned pregnancy can take their toll, so while feeling sad or unsettled is common, it should soon subside.
- There's no reason why you should stop yourself from feeling sad when a pregnancy ends, for whatever reason. Grief and sadness are normal, healthy emotions and are different from depression.
- Talking about your feelings with friends, family or a professional can really help. Although you might feel you don't 'deserve' sympathy because you chose to have an abortion, there are people who understand that this was a difficult decision and that you deserve as much help and support as possible.

Psychologist's view

'If you experience powerful feelings of guilt or sadness, it's important to explore the reasons why you feel this way. In your worst moments, you might not feel like you deserve happiness, but you need to remind yourself that your decision was taken with a great deal of wisdom and care. Whilst I wouldn't advise you to indulge yourself by imagining what might have been, you must be honest and acknowledge your feelings if you're not 100%. Keeping a diary of your recovery may also be helpful so you can see how far you are moving forward emotionally.' Dr Sandra L. Wheatley PhD CPsychol, independent psychology consultant.

Depression

If two months have passed since your abortion and you are still feeling down, distressed or anxious, make an appointment with your GP. Although there is no direct link between abortion and depression, the event could be a catalyst for other problems in your life. It's also important to remember that depression can be triggered by innumerable issues and physical changes and, according to the Office of National Statistics, depression occurs in one in 10 adults or 10% of the British population at any one time.

Symptoms of depression can include:

- Losing interest in normal activities and hobbies.
- Feeling tired and lacking energy.
- Having problems sleeping and getting up in the morning.
- Poor appetite.
- Problems concentrating and feeling indecisive.
- Losing interest in sex.
- Feeling restless, irritable, tense and anxious.
- Losing your self confidence and avoiding others.
- Feeling guilty, hopeless or useless.
- Thinking about suicide.

If you think you might be depressed, remind yourself that depression is an illness; it is not your fault and you will get better, no matter how hopeless you feel. Talk to your GP as soon as you can or contact the following organisations:

- Mind (www.mind.org.uk).
- Depression Alliance (www.depressionalliance.org).
- Mental Health Foundation (www.mentalhealth.org.uk).

Helping yourself

If you feel sad, down or stressed following an abortion, there is lots you can do to help yourself feel better, as well as seeking any professional help you might need:

- Avoid alcohol and drugs as they can intensify your emotions and make you feel worse in the long run.
- If you're not sleeping well, try napping during the day to recharge your batteries as sleep deprivation can affect your mood and wellbeing.
- Some gentle exercise can trigger the release of endorphins – the 'feel-good' chemicals naturally manufactured in the brain. You might not feel like running a marathon, but even short walks make a difference.

'A termination can sometimes leave women with emotional issues. If a woman feels psychologically affected, we can offer support within the practice, either talking things over with a GP or a counsellor, if available. We can also refer to an outside clinic. If a woman is under 25, we are able to ask Brook for their expertise and follow on support.' Dr Charlotte Zoltonos, GP.

Dealing with guilt

Guilt is a very common emotion to experience after an abortion:

- Many women keep their abortion a secret and this carries a sense of shame, particularly if it involves lying to friends and family.
- Some women feel guilty about ending the pregnancy, dwelling on thoughts of an unborn baby and worrying that they have somehow ruined their chances of having another child.

Like all emotions, it's easiest to deal with guilt by talking it through. You may find that your partner feels the same way as you, and sharing your feelings can lift the burden. Talking to other women who have experienced an abortion can also help as they may be able to relate to your feelings and reassure you that they will pass.

Although feeling guilty is completely normal, try not to be too hard on yourself. You don't deserve to feel bad or anxious, or to be made to feel guilty by others. Seeking reassurance from someone supportive can help you to overcome your feelings.

Remember that guilt is a normal emotion – and it's one that is regularly experienced by mothers, who constantly worry if they're doing the right thing. It's likely that if you had gone ahead with the pregnancy you would still be experiencing feelings of guilt, just for different reasons.

Moving on

Moving forward with your partner

After an abortion you may find that your relationship is strengthened – or strained. You may deal with the abortion in different ways:

- You may not think that your partner appreciates what you're going through, or feel that he expects you to get over it too quickly. Try to share honestly what you're feeling so he understands, and be clear about how you want him to support you.
- If your partner feels upset, remember that he is entitled to feel that way. Although you went through the physical experience of abortion, don't underestimate the impact it has on those around you. Discuss your feelings openly and resist any urge to sweep emotions under the carpet; leaving matters unresolved can make the situation worse.
- For some women, an abortion initiates sexual problems, particularly if fear of another unwanted pregnancy changes the way they feel about their partner or sex in general. If you're struggling to get through the issue, consider seeking help from a sex therapist or relationship counsellor, or ask a third party you both trust to mediate.

Moving forward with friends and family

Like the rest of society, friends and family will react to your abortion in different ways:

- They could offer help and support, they may be angry with you or expect you to carry on as normal without making a fuss.
- Many women don't feel they are given the opportunity to acknowledge their grief or bereavement after an abortion. Even when a pregnancy is terminated for medical reasons, friends and family may sympathise because a woman went through an abortion, rather than comforting her in her loss.
- It's important to share your feelings with friends and family so you can all move on. If their reactions have upset you, it's important to acknowledge that so resentment doesn't build.
- Communication is the key to any healthy relationship, so even if friends and family don't want to talk now, encourage them to express their feelings when they're ready.

Just as you have the right to make choices, your friends and family have the right to their opinion. You can't force them to agree with your decision. You can, however, ask for their help and support as you recover.

Telling children about your abortion

Abortion can be a difficult subject to tackle with children; deciding whether or not to tell them is a personal decision. Much depends on whether they knew you were pregnant. If they didn't, you might decide not to tell them at all or to tell them when they're older.

- If your child knew you were pregnant, ask yourself how he or she will react and how much they can be expected to understand. If they get upset when you explain, assure them that it's okay to feel sad and angry. It will help them if you show patience and understanding, and answering their questions will allow them to come to terms with what has happened.
- If you have older children, it helps to explain the procedure to them.
- If your abortion happened a long time ago and you now have teenage

children, you may decide to tell them in order to initiate a conversation about contraception. This works well for some families, but do be aware that teenagers can react unexpectedly.

- Exercise care and caution when discussing abortion, testing the water as you go. Announcing you had an abortion in the midst of an argument is definitely not advisable, and just because abortion was the right choice for you, it doesn't mean that it will be the right path for them if they are ever faced with an unplanned pregnancy.

Looking back

'I'd suffered infertility for 20 years and felt happy with the way my life was going. When I unexpectedly got pregnant, I instantly thought about abortion. I wrote lists of pros and cons and spoke to helpline counsellors, my GP, husband and parents. Ultimately, I feared wanting a child one day and not being able to – and I couldn't end a pregnancy that, after years of infertility, felt like a miracle. I had a thousand regrets during pregnancy and suffered from post natal depression. On bad days, I did wonder if I should have had an abortion. Looking after a child is hard, hard work, with huge highs and terribly dark lows. However, my daughter is a never-ending source of wonderment and love. I have no problem with the fact that I considered an abortion and want to be open with my daughter about it when she's old enough.' Eva, 38.

If your pregnancy was unplanned but you decided to go on and become a parent, you should never feel guilty because you considered all your options before you came to your decision. Even women who plan their pregnancies for years may have doubts when they actually get pregnant and consider having an abortion.

'I had an abortion at 19 after a drunken one night stand. I'm not sorry I had the termination, but being in that position is still a source of great regret. I occasionally think what might have been and my abortion was 21 years ago.'

Carol, 40.

Preventing another unwanted pregnancy

You can conceive as early as one or two weeks after an abortion, so contraception is essential if you want to avoid another unwanted pregnancy.

- Whatever your age, you can get free and confidential advice about sex and contraception from a local family planning clinic, NHS sexual health clinic (GUM), young person's sexual health centre, Brook (for under-25s) or your GP.

- You can start taking the pill as soon as you have had an abortion, but you should also use condoms while taking antibiotics.
- You can have a long-acting contraceptive like Depo-Provera, IUCD, IUS or Implanon fitted at the same time as you have an abortion.
- Whatever method of contraception you choose, it's important to use condoms too as they can protect you from STIs as well as pregnancy. Condoms are free from a local youth or family planning clinic and some doctors, or you can buy them at a local chemist, shop, supermarket, petrol station or vending machine.
- Many abortion clinics offer sterilisation and vasectomies as well as abortion. You can discuss the pros and cons of this operation with the clinic, but this may be a good option if you're absolutely sure you don't want any more children, or certain you never want to start a family.

'I hope that when my daughter grows up she'll be open with me about sex and not find herself in the same situation I did. If she ever did have an abortion, I would be there for her, holding her hand when she came round.'

Diana, 32.

Summing Up

- You may experience a range of emotions after an abortion, but you are less likely to have regrets if you made an informed and considered decision.
- Guilt, grief and sadness are all normal responses to the end of a pregnancy. With a good network of support, and a little self-kindness, you can overcome these emotions and move on.
- There are always people you can turn to after an abortion who will help you recover without judging you or making you feel guilty about the decision you made. If this isn't a partner, family member or friend, it could be a GP, a counsellor or a family planning clinic worker.

Glossary

Contraception: any method used to stop a woman getting pregnant, including condoms, the pill and the coil.

Depression: a common mental disorder with a range of symptoms that can lead to substantial impairments in an individual's ability to take care of his or her everyday responsibilities.

Guilt: a feeling of responsibility or remorse for some kind of wrongdoing that may be real or imagined.

Infertility: being unable to conceive a child.

Sex therapist: a sex therapist is specially trained to help people work through their sexual problems.

Sterilisation: a permanent form of contraception where a woman's fallopian tubes (the tubes between the ovary and the womb) are cut or blocked with rings or clips.

Vasectomy: a permanent method of contraception for a man which prevents the release of sperm when he ejaculates (comes).

'There are excellent support services for younger women, but there's a gap for women over 25. These women can be most distressed by abortion because they feel embarrassed and humiliated and may need additional help to recover.'

Ann Furedi, chief executive, BPAS.

Chapter Thirteen

Frequently Asked Questions

I've done a positive pregnancy test – am I definitely pregnant?

Pregnancy tests detect a hormone that is present in your body if you are pregnant, so a false positive is very unlikely. An ultrasound scan can confirm your pregnancy if you have a positive test but don't think you can be pregnant.

Will a doctor talk to my parents on my behalf?

If you're under 16, your doctor may encourage you to involve your parents in your decision-making process. They may also offer to talk to your parents with you about an unplanned pregnancy and all your options. A doctor should never talk to your parents without your consent unless he or she believes that you or another person is at risk.

How quickly can I access an abortion?

Waiting times for NHS treatment vary according to where you live. If you can attend an independent family planning or abortion clinic, you may still be able to access NHS treatment but receive it much more quickly.

After being referred by a clinic or GP, you should never have to wait more than two weeks for your first consultation, and once the decision to go ahead has been agreed with two doctors, you should never have to wait for more than two weeks for your abortion. You should be seen without any delay if you need an abortion for urgent medical reasons.

Will an early medical abortion (EMA) definitely work?

In some cases, an EMA fails to remove a pregnancy. Most clinics will advise you to take a pregnancy test three weeks after the procedure to check. If the EMA has not worked, you can choose to have the treatment again or have a surgical abortion. According to the Royal College of Obstetricians and Gynaecologists (RCOG), medical abortion is more successful than surgical abortion before the seventh week of pregnancy.

How many abortions fail?

Overall, just over two out of every 1,000 women who have a surgical abortion continue to be pregnant. Different studies show different failure rates for medical abortions, with figures ranging from two in every 1,000 to 14 in every 1,000 (Royal College of Obstetricians and Gynaecologists).

What happens if I'm RhD negative?

If your blood type is RhD negative (which will be detected when you have your blood tests – the majority of people are RhD positive), you'll usually be offered an anti-D injection after your abortion. This is to prevent miscarriage in future pregnancies. Your healthcare provider should give you information about anti-D injections after your blood tests, if necessary. However, if you already know you're RhD negative, there's no harm in mentioning it.

Is abortion safer than being pregnant?

For most women, an abortion is safer than carrying a pregnancy and giving birth. No medical or surgical procedure is entirely risk free, but the earlier in pregnancy you have an abortion, the safer it is. Your doctor or nurse will explain any risks and complications relating to the type of abortion you're having. If you have any particular concerns, let them know so they can reassure you.

Will abortion be painful?

Most abortions will cause some pain or discomfort – this depends on the stage of pregnancy and the individual. Pain relief should always be available.

Can any other procedures be carried out without my knowledge?

Sometimes extra procedures are necessary at the time of an operation to save a person's life or prevent serious harm to their health. Your doctor or nurse should advise you about this when you consent to treatment. You have a right to say whether there are any procedures you don't want the surgeon to carry out and to be fully informed about your healthcare and any decisions that need to be made. Your wishes should always be taken into account.

Can I sign myself out of hospital if I don't want to stay overnight?

Most clinics now offer abortion services as day-care – an overnight stay is unusual for under 20 weeks. Most clinics ask you to stay for a short time after treatment and you'll be discharged once your healthcare providers are satisfied that you're recovering well and there are no complications. It's always best to follow their advice. If you have an abortion between 20 and 24 weeks, an overnight stay is more likely and may be necessary to complete the treatment safely. If you want to sign yourself out, speak to the nurses looking after you and they will advise you. If you change your mind about an abortion, you can leave the clinic without being treated right up until the procedure actually begins – never feel obliged to go through with it if you still feel unsure.

Can I complain if I've been unfairly treated by a nurse or doctor?

Yes. Initially, if you have an issue with a particular member of staff, you could ask to speak to the clinic manager or a senior practitioner at the hospital – a good organisation or healthcare provider will always appreciate your feedback, whether it's good or bad. If you would rather speak to someone outside the clinic, you can contact the Healthcare Commission (www.healthcarecommission.org.uk).

Should I allow my children to come to the clinic?

This is a personal decision and you will also need to consult the clinic. Much depends on the treatment you're having, the age of your child(ren) and how well they will cope and behave in the clinic. You also need to take the feelings of other clients into account; bringing children, especially young ones, into this environment may be upsetting for women who are having an abortion. If the clinic does not allow children and you have childcare issues, ask for advice as they may be able to suggest local crèche or childcare facilities.

Is there a link between abortion and breast cancer?

Breakthrough Breast Cancer (www.breakthrough.org.uk) reports that the World Health Organisation and the Royal College of Obstetricians and Gynaecologists have independently reviewed the scientific evidence on a link between abortion and breast cancer. Both organisations have concluded that abortion does not increase the risk of developing breast cancer.

Will abortion make me infertile?

There's no evidence that abortion will affect your fertility. Sadly, some women are so worried about this that they have sex without contraception after an abortion to 'test' their fertility. There is no reason to do this and it's worth noting that multiple abortions may slightly increase the risk of miscarriage in future pregnancies.

Will my abortion be included on my medical record?

If you're referred for NHS treatment by your GP or give permission for your doctor to be contacted, your abortion may go on your medical record. If you receive private treatment or have an NHS abortion via a family planning clinic or young person's clinic like Brook, your GP doesn't have to be involved and the treatment will not be included on your medical record.

If I get pregnant again, do I need to mention my abortion?

If the abortion isn't on your medical record, you don't have to disclose it. However, when you are booked in for antenatal care you will usually be asked if you have been pregnant before. Although you can withhold this information, you'll get the best care possible by sharing your complete medical history with your healthcare team. It's worth noting that if you do decide to disclose the information, it will be logged in the bundle of notes you carry with you during pregnancy and after the birth. If you don't want your partner or family members to see this, talk to your midwife to see if it can be left out of your notes.

How much will my abortion cost?

NHS services are free but you will have to arrange your own transport to the clinic or hospital. Costs for private treatment vary depending on the individual clinic and the stage of the pregnancy. According to Private Healthcare UK (www.privatehealth.co.uk), an initial consultation costs between £50-£70 and the procedure will cost between £350 and £750 up to 19 weeks of pregnancy.

Can I stop my partner or daughter from having an abortion?

Having an abortion is wholly a woman's decision and all legal challenges made by men have failed to date. You cannot prevent your daughter from having an abortion and, even if she is under 16, it is highly unlikely that you can legally prevent her from having treatment. Similarly, you cannot force a woman to have an abortion if you are a parent or partner. However you feel about her decision, what she really needs is your support and care.

Do I have to have a male doctor?

The majority of abortion surgeons in England, Scotland and Wales are men, but they are supported by a range of healthcare workers who may be male or female. An EMA is a nurse-led procedure, but nurses are male as well as female. You may be able to request a female nurse depending on the staff available at the hospital or clinic. If there are no female abortion surgeons in your area, you can't demand to be treated by a woman but you can ask if a female member of staff can be present at all times to support you.

When should I start using contraception again?

You should start using contraception straight away. It is safe – and may be advisable, depending on your circumstances – to have a long-acting contraceptive fitted at the same time as your abortion.

Summing Up

- If you decide to have an abortion, information is the key to overcoming any fears you have about the procedure or the impact it may have on your physical and emotional wellbeing.
- Asking your healthcare team any questions you have, no matter how trivial they seem, will help you get through an abortion positively.
- If your questions have not been answered either by your healthcare team or this book, don't hesitate to seek further advice from the specialist agencies and charities listed throughout this book and in the help section.

Help List

Abortion Rights

18 Ashwin Street, London, E8 3DL
Tel: 020 7923 9792
www.abortionrights.org.uk
The national pro-choice campaign. You can email enquiries through the website.

Antenatal Results and Choices (ARC)

73 Charlotte Street, London, W1T 4PN
Tel: 0207 631 0285 (helpline)
info@arc-uk.org
www.arc-uk.org
A national UK charity providing non-directive support and information to expectant and bereaved parents throughout and after the antenatal screening and testing process.

BabyCentre

www.babycentre.co.uk
A resource and community dedicated to helping new and expectant parents find information, support and reassurance.

British Association for Adoption and Fostering (BAAF)

BAAF Head Office, Saffron House, 6-10 Kirby Street, London, EC1N 8TS
Tel: 020 7421 2600 (enquiries)
mail@baaf.org.uk
www.baaf.org.uk
A leading UK charity working with everyone involved in adoption and fostering across the UK.

British Association for Counselling and Psychotherapy

BACP House, 15 St John's Business Park, Lutterworth, Leicestershire, LE17 4HB
Tel: 01455 883300 (general enquiries)
Tel: 01455 883 316 (BACP information helpdesk)
bacp@bacp.co.uk
www.bacp.co.uk
A service helping potential clients find a suitable counsellor in their particular area. Call the information desk for help with finding a counsellor.

British Pregnancy Advisory Service (BPAS)

Head Office, 20 Timothys Bridge Road, Stratford Enterprise Park, Stratford-upon-Avon, Warwickshire, CV37 9BF
Tel: 08457 30 40 30 (action line)
info@bpas.org
www.bpas.org
The leading provider of UK abortion services, with a national network of consultation centres and clinics. Call the action line to discuss your options with a trained BPAS member.

Brook

421 Highgate Studios, 53-79 Highgate Road, London, NW5 1TL
Tel: 0808 802 1234 (confidential helpline)
admin@brookcentres.org.uk (general enquiries)
www.brook.org.uk
Brook provides free and confidential sexual health advice and services to young people under 25. Visit the website for details of your local Brook centre.

Calthorpe Clinic

4 Arthur Road, Edgbaston, Birmingham, B15 2UL
Tel: 0121 455 7585
www.calthorpe-clinic.co.uk
A clinic that has been providing surgical and medical terminations for 40 years.

Child Bereavement Charity

Aston House, West Wycombe, High Wycombe, Bucks, HP14 3AG

Tel: 01494 446648 (support and information)
support@childbereavement.org.uk
www.childbereavement.org.uk
Child Bereavement Charity provides specialised support, information and training to all those affected both when a child dies and when a child is bereaved. The site covers miscarriage, stillbirth and pregnancies terminated due to foetal abnormality.

ChildLine

Tel: 0800 1111 (24 hour helpline)
www.childline.org.uk
ChildLine is the free confidential helpline for children and young people in the UK – you can talk to them about anything.

Community Legal Advice

Tel: 0845 345 4 345
www.communitylegaladvice.org.uk
Free, confidential and independent legal advice for residents of England and Wales.

Connexions Direct

Tel: 0808 001 3219
www.connexions-direct.com
Offers advice on education, careers, housing, money, health and relationships for 13-19-year-olds in the UK.

Cruse Bereavement Care

PO Box 800, Richmond, Surrey, TW9 1RG
Tel: 0844 477 9400 (helpline)
helpline@cruse.org.uk
www.crusebereavementcare.co.uk
Cruse promotes the wellbeing of bereaved people and enables anyone bereaved by death to understand their grief and cope with their loss. Free leaflets can be downloaded from the website.

Cruse Northern Ireland

Piney Ridge, Knockbracken Healthcare Park, Saintfield Road, Belfast, BT8 8BH
Tel: 028 90 792419
northern.ireland@cruse.org.uk

Department for Work and Pensions

www.dwp.gov.uk
Information on maternity and family benefits, including child support.

Depression Alliance

212 Spitfire Studios, 63-71 Collier Street, London, N1 9BE
Tel: 0845 123 23 0
information@depressionalliance.org
www.depressionalliance.org
With offices in England and a sister charity in Scotland, Depression Alliance has a network of self-help groups.

Directgov

www.direct.gov.uk
The official government website including information on health services, money and benefits.

Doctors for a Woman's Choice on Abortion (DWCA)

19 Vincent Terrace, London, N1 8HN
Tel: 020 7837 7635
www.dwca.org
DWCA is a group of doctors who believe that the law should be changed to allow a woman to decide for herself whether or not to have an abortion.

Education for Choice

The Print House,18 Ashwin Street, London, E8 3DL
Tel: 020 7249 3535
efc@efc.org.uk
www.efc.org.uk

The only UK-based educational charity dedicated to enabling young people to make informed choices about pregnancy and abortion.

fpa

Tel: 0845 122 8690 (helpline)
www.fpa.org.uk
fpa (Family Planning Association) is the UK's leading sexual health charity. It aims to enable people in the UK to make informed choices about sex and enjoy sexual health.

fpa Northern Ireland

3rd Floor Ascot House, 24-31 Shaftesbury Square, Belfast, BT2 7DB
Tel: 0845 122 8687 (helpline)

Gingerbread

Tel: 0800 018 5026
www.gingerbread.org.uk
An organisation for lone parent families.

Healthcare Commission

Tel: 0845 601 3012 (helpline)
www.healthcarecommission.org.uk
The Healthcare Commission is the independent watchdog for healthcare in England, assessing and reporting on the quality and safety of services provided by the NHS and the independent healthcare sector.

Marie Stopes

Tel: 0845 300 8090
services@mariestopes.org.uk
www.mariestopes.org.uk
Provides sexual and reproductive healthcare services.

Mental Health Foundation

9th Floor, Sea Containers House, 20 Upper Ground, London, SE1 9QB
mhf@mhf.org.uk

www.mentalhealth.org.uk
A UK charity helping people survive, recover from and prevent mental health problems. They do not provide advice on individual mental health problems, but information can be found on their website.

Mental Health Foundation Scotland

Merchants House, 30 George Square, Glasgow, G2 1EG
scotland@mhf.org.uk

MIND

Tel: 0845 766 0163 (information line)
www.mind.org.uk
The national association for mental health.

Mother 35 Plus

Tel: 07804 631585
www.mothers35plus.co.uk
The UK's leading website devoted to 'late motherhood'. No medical advice offered.

National Domestic Violence Helpline UK

Tel: 0808 2000 247
www.womensaid.org.uk
A free, national helpline service for women experiencing domestic violence, their family, friends, colleagues and others calling on their behalf. The helpline is run in partnership with Women's Aid and Refuge.

Net Doctor

www.netdoctor.co.uk
An independent medical information and health website.

Netmums

www.netmums.com
A local online network for parents.

NHS Direct

Tel: 0845 4647
www.nhsdirect.nhs.uk
Health advice and information.

Parentline Plus

520 Highgate Studios, 53-79 Highgate Road, Kentish Town, London, NW5 1TL
Tel: 0808 800 2222
www.parentlineplus.org.uk
A national charity working for, and with, parents.

Relate

Tel: 0300 100 1234
www.relate.org.uk
Offers advice, relationship counselling, sex therapy, workshops, mediation, consultations and support.

R U Thinking?

Tel: 0800 28 29 30
www.ruthinking.co.uk
Everything young people need to know about sex and relationships.

Sands

28 Portland Place, London, W1B 1LY
Tel: 020 7436 5881
www.uk-sands.org
Sands is an organisation which offers support when a baby dies during pregnancy or after birth.

theSite.org

www.thesite.org
TheSite.org aims to be the first place young adults turn to when they need support and guidance through life.

Voice for Choice

www.vfc.org.uk
Voice for Choice is a national coalition of organisations working alongside the All Party Parliamentary Pro-Choice and Sexual Health Group to campaign for a woman's choice on abortion.